A hat for this
a hat for that
but nothing
to wear,
imagine that!

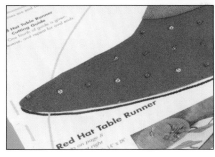

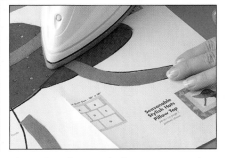

sheet that your designs can be pressed directly onto, cooled and peeled off intact. They can then be placed on your quilt, shirt or wall hanging and pressed in place.

Lay your pattern on your ironing board. Lay the Pressing sheet on top. Peel the paper off the applique pieces and lay them directly on the pressing

sheet, lined up with the pattern underneath. Press for 2-3 seconds to fuse. Cool. Peel applique off as one piece.

Position on the quilt top and press to permanently fuse the fabric applique piece to the quilt.

In order to successfully complete these projects, you must have basic quilting skills, accurate cutting skills

e.
ou
te
d.

Have Fun!

Red hats on purple fabric by
Marcus Brothers Textiles
www.MarcusBrothers.com

A hat for this
a hat for that
but nothing
to wear,
imagine that!

Red Hats Abound

Seasonable Stylish Hats

Turn individual blocks into attractive pillow tops using scraps of fabric.

All tops are assembled the same way - add side sashings, top and bottom sashings, side borders, top and bottom borders.

patterns on pages 18 - 29

pillow instructions on page 17

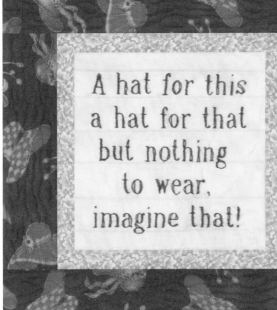

Red and Purple Hat Pillow Top

FINISHED SIZE: 18" x 22"
CUTTING:
Creme/Ecru for block (8½" x 12½")
2½" wide Creme/Tan sashing : 2 sides 8½"; top/bottom 16½"
3½" wide Purple border: 2 sides 12½"; top/bottom 22½"
Backing fabric and batting (20" x 24")

Poem Pillow Top

Poem by Sarah Haynes
FINISHED SIZE: 18" x 18"
CUTTING:
Creme/Ecru for block (10½" x 10½")
1½" wide Creme/Tan sashing: 2 sides 10½"; top/bottom 12½"
3½" wide Purple border: 2 sides 12½" long
                top/bottom 18½" long
Backing fabric and batting (20" x 20")

Red and Pink Hat Pillow Top

FINISHED SIZE: 16" x 21"
CUTTING:
Creme/Ecru for block (10½" x 15½")
1½" wide Creme/Tan sashing: 2 sides 10½";
                top/bottom 17½"
2½" wide Purple border: 2 sides 12½" long
                top/bottom 21½" long
Backing fabric and batting (18" x 23")

☕ea for Two
Tea Party Quilt

Tea time can be elegantly simple or simply elegant, depending on your mood. Choose fabrics that say, "I'll have the staff bring out the cucumber sandwiches" or "How about a cookie?" Either way, you will enjoy making the wall hanging and pillow tops. Tea for 2 poem by Sarah Haynes.

patterns on pages 34 - 41
pillow instructions on page 17

All Pillow Tops

FINISHED SIZE: 14½" x 14½"
CUTTING :
Creme/Ecru for block (9½" x 9½")
1½" wide sashing : 2 sides 9½" long;
                top/bottom 11½" long
2¼" wide border: 2 sides 11½" long;
                top/bottom 15" long
Backing fabric and batting (16" x 16")

Tea for 2
a cup for you
2 for tea
a cup for me

Tea Time
Tea Pot Table Runner

Make this Tea Pot table runner for the special friend or family member who collects tea pots. It's also a great Mother's Day gift idea for your Girl Scout troop.

patterns on page 37

Red Hats at Christmas
Poinsettia Table Runner

Poinsettias are the perfect winter flower. Bring your Red Hat decor to the Christmas party with this Poinsettia Hat table runner. Apply this pattern to a tea towel to extend your theme into the kitchen. Have you thought of putting your Red Hat design on a holiday apron or jumper or vest?

Wouldn't it be fun to go caroling decked out in hats and coordinating attire? Let this design kick-start your ideas for extending the use of this great pattern. As a group, make tote bags to carry all your holiday shopping...oops, I forgot! You already made all your gifts from this book, so there's no shopping to do. Oh well, you still have to go to the grocery store. You can show off your tote bag there. In the meantime, decorate the house with "hat-titude" and have a wonderful season.

patterns on page 19

Gardener's Delight
Garden Club Wall Quilt

All winter long I think about my garden. Reading and planning, I can't wait for that last thaw. This garden quilt captures the joy of working outdoors.

patterns on pages 42 - 51

pillow instructions on page 17

Watering Can Pillow Top
FINISHED SIZE: 16" x 18"
CUTTING:
Creme/Ecru for block (10½" x 12½")
1½" wide Purple sashing: 2 sides 12½" long; top/bottom 12½" long
2½" wide Green border: 2 sides 14½" long; top/bottom 16½" long
Backing fabric and batting (18" x 20")

Pink Spring Flowers Pillow Top
FINISHED SIZE: 15" x 17"
CUTTING:
Creme/Ecru for block (7½" x 9½")
1½" wide Green sashing: 2 sides 9½" long; top/bottom 9½" long
1½" wide Purple sashing: 2 sides 11½" long; top/bottom 11½" long
2½" wide Green border: 2 sides 13½" long; top/bottom 15½" long
Backing fabric and batting (17" x 19")

Red Flowers and Garden Tools Pillow Top
FINISHED SIZE: 15" x 28"
CUTTING:
Creme/Ecru for block (8½" x 21½")
1½" wide Purple sashing: 2 sides 8½" long; top/bottom 23½" long
3" wide border: 2 sides 10½" long; top/bottom 28½" long
Backing fabric and batting (17" x 30")

𝒫icking Flowers

Friends and Flowers Wall Hanging

Put a little humor in your sunroom or patio with this Picking Flowers wall hanging. Have fun stitching these words by poet Sarah Haynes. This project is small and simple, so you will still have time for both friends and flowers.

For those who work with scout troops or youth groups, this pattern provides enough techniques for needle arts badges. This wall hanging would make a wonderful service project to brighten up a retirement home, hospital room, or shelter. This project easily turns into a tote bag. If you border the block with several fabrics, it turns into a crib size quilt for the Linus Quilt Project or the ABC Quilt program.

patterns are on page 53 - 55

Planting Flowers
Flower Table Runner

Here's another little quilt that could be used as a dresser scarf. If you make it a little smaller, it becomes a lovely place mat. Make a set of 4 for a Spring wedding or shower gift with flowers in the bride's favorite colors. Or, cut the design down the middle to get both sides of a tote bag. The gift possibilities are numerous. No matter what you create, this project will brighten your day and your decor.

patterns on page 45

All Things Divine
A Lady's Sampler

What is the perfect gift for a wonderful lady?
Accessories, of course! And Chocolate!
Have fun with this whimsical wall hanging.
You'll love the squares as pillow tops too!
patterns on pages 56 - 63
pillow instructions on page 17

High Heel Slipper Pillow Top
FINISHED SIZE: 14" x 15"
CUTTING:
Purple print for block (6½" x 7½")
2" wide Pink sashing: 2 sides 6½" long; top/bottom 10½" long
3" wide Red border: 2 sides 9½" long; top/bottom 15½" long
Backing fabric and batting (16" x 17")

Red Hat Tea Pot Pillow Top
FINISHED SIZE: 15" x 15"
CUTTING:
Ecru print for block (7½" x 7½")
2" wide Pink sashing: 2 sides 7½" long; top/bottom 10½" long
3" wide Red border: 2 sides 10½" long; top/bottom 15½" long
Backing fabric and batting (17" x 17")

Pillow tops are all assembled the same way. Make the block according to the quilt directions. Add side sashings. Add top and bottom sashings. Add side borders. Add top and bottom borders. Make backing and quilt as desired. Then, turn to the easy pillow assembly directions on page 17.

Box of Chocolates Pillow Top
FINISHED SIZE: 15" x 15"
CUTTING:
Purple print for block (9½" x 9½")
1½" wide Pink sashing: 2 sides 9½" long;
        top/bottom 11½" long
2½" wide Red border: 2 sides 11½" long;
        top/bottom 15½" long
Backing fabric and batting (17" x 17")

ℬoudoir Decor
Red Hat Table Runner

Table runners aren't just for the dining table. Decorate a dresser or table in the bedroom with a Red Hat table runner. Apply this pattern to a couple of pillowcases. Make a neck roll pillow in a coordinating color. Soon, you will have a whole bedroom that expresses a bright, happy "Hat-titude"! It's easy to get carried away with curtains and dust ruffles. Frame one of these quilted projects and hang it on the wall. Don't be surprised if your design leaks into other connecting rooms. For example, the connecting bath could use some coordinating fabric on the bottom of the towels. Let yourself get carried away and have a lot of fun!

patterns are on page 24 - 25

Hat-titude Basics

Pillow Instructions

DESIGN BLOCK:
- Make the block according to the quilt directions.
- Add side sashings. Add top and bottom sashings.
- Add side borders. Add top and bottom borders.
- Back and quilt the block as desired.
- Square up the block.

BACK OF PILLOW:
- Measure the length and width of the pillow top.
- The pillow back will be cut in 2 pieces of equal size.
- To find the width, divide the pillow top width by 2. Add 4".
- The length will be the same. Cut both back pieces.
- Turn back $^1/_4$" along the left edge of one piece. Fold back $1^1/_2$" again along the same edge. Topstitch across the fabric through all layers close to the edge of the first fold.
- Repeat hems along the right edge of the other piece.
- Lay the pillow front flat, right side facing. Lay one back piece on top of the front so right sides face, aligning raw edges. If you used a print, make certain the motifs on both pieces are right side up.

- Lay the other back piece on the pillow top, right sides facing, aligning raw edges. Make certain the motifs on the piece are right side up. The hemmed edges of the back pieces will overlap down the center of pillow.
- Pin back pieces in place on top of the pillow front, sew pillow pieces together around the raw edges.
- Turn the pillow to the right side through the back of the opening.
- Topstitch 'in the ditch' around the joining seam between the borders and the pillow center.
- Insert pillow into back opening.

Pillow Back Diagram

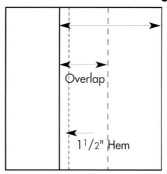

Overlap

$1^1/_2$" Hem

Stitch Guide

Whip Stitch

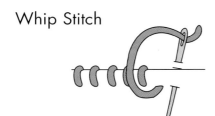

Insert the needle under a few fibers of one layer of fabric. Bring the needle up through the other layer of fabric. Use this stitch to attach the folded raw edges of fabric to the back of pieces or to attach bindings around the edges of quilts and coverlets.

Back Stitch

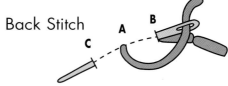

Insert the needle up at A, and down at B. Come back up through the bottom at C. Repeat.

French Knot

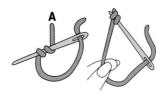

Come up at A. Wrap the floss around the needle 2 to 3 times. Insert the needle close to A. Hold the floss and pull the needle through the loops gently.

Quilt Binding Instructions

1. Cut 2" wide binding strips across the width of the fabric.
2. Sew enough strips together, end-to-end, to go around the quilt. Press seams open.
3. Fold the strip in half lengthwise, with wrong sides together.
4. Pin the raw edge of the binding strip to align with the raw edges of the top/batting/backing sandwich.
5. Machine sew binding strip in place, stitching through all layers.
6. At the corner, leave the needle in place through the fabrics and fold binding up straight. Fold it up and over into a mitered corner.
7. Fold the folded edge of the binding to the back. Whip Stitch the edge in place. Miter the corners on the front and on the back. Stitch corners closed.

Fold strip in half, wrong sides facing.

Align all raw edges.

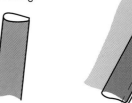

Leave the needle in position at the corner. Fold binding up and back to miter.

Seasonable Stylish Hats

photo on page 3
patterns on pages 19 - 29
poem by Sarah Haynes

FINISHED SIZE:
36" x 36"

MATERIALS:
⅔ yard for border and binding
7 fat quarters Creme/ Ecru for blocks
¼ yard Creme/Tan for sashing
1⅛ yards backing fabric
¼ yard cuts or scraps for applique: 7 shades Red, 3 shades Dark Red, 2 shades Gold, 2 shades Purple, 2 shades Green, Pink, White or Natural, Orange, Navy
DMC Pearl Cotton #5 (Purple, Gold) • Steam-A-Seam II fusible web • *Warm & Natural* Cotton batting • Disappearing pen

CUTTING:

Cut Ecru/Creme BLOCKS
2   8½" x 12½" for A and B
2   9½" x 10½" for C and E
1   10½" x 10½" for D
1   10½" x 13½" for F
1   10½" x 15½" for G
Cut Creme/Tan SASHING
3 strips   2½" x 8½" for Blocks A, B
4 strips   1½" x 10½" for Blocks D, G
2 strips   1½" x 30½" goes between rows 1-2 and 2-3
Cut from OUTER BORDER fabric
2 strips   3½" x 30½" for sides
2 strips   3½" x 36½" for top and bottom
Cut 2" strips of binding and sew together for 150"

INSTRUCTIONS:

1. Cut out all blocks and border strips.
2. Trace hat poem on 10½" x 10½" center block with a disappearing pen.
3. Back Stitch the words using Purple pearl cotton. Press.
4. Arrange blocks as shown in chart 1.
5. Sew in rows across, with right sides together, pressing each seam as you go.
6. **Row 1**: Sew a 2½" x 8½" Creme/Tan Sashing strip to both sides of Block A.
7. Sew a 2½" x 8½" strip to the right side of Block B.
8. Sew Block B to Block A.
9. Sew a 1½" x 30½" Creme/Tan Sashing strip across the bottom of Row 1.
10. **Row 2**: Sew a 1½" x 10½" strip to both sides of Block D.
11. Sew Block C and E to each side of Block D.
12. Sew a 1½" x 30½" Creme/Tan Sashing strip across the bottom of Row 2.
13. **Row 3**: Sew a 1½" x 10½" strip to both sides of Block G.
14. Sew Block F to the left side of Block G.
15. Sew Row 2 to the bottom of Row 1.
16. Sew Row 3 to the bottom of Row 2.
17. Sew the 3½" x 30½" side borders to each side, press, then sew on the 3½" x 36½" top & bottom borders.

APPLIQUE:

1. Trace applique patterns in reverse onto fusible web.
2. Where noted, label each piece.
3. Press each drawn piece to fabric according to pattern and cut out each shape.
4. Use the pattern to assemble each hat.
5. Lay hats on each block and center as needed.
6. Press in place following manufacturer's directions.
7. Follow the directions under "finishing up" on page 66.

Chart 1 - Row Assembly

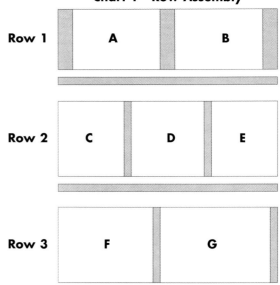

Row 1 — A   B
Row 2 — C   D   E
Row 3 — F   G

Borders and Sashings

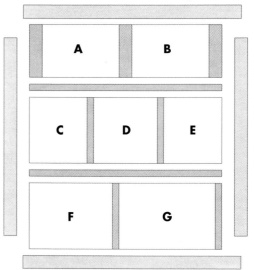

A   B
C   D   E
F   G

Finished Quilt Size - 36" x 36"

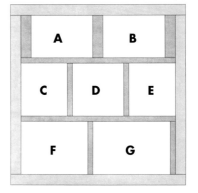

A   B
C   D   E
F   G

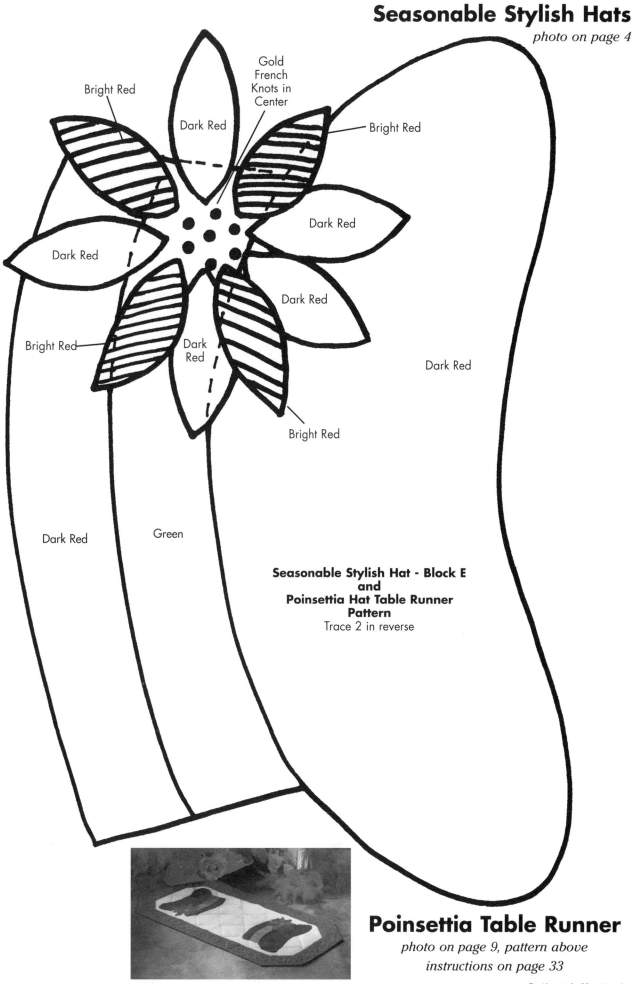

Bright Red

Gold
French
Knots in
Center

Dark Red

Bright Red

Bright Red

Dark Red

Dark Red

Dark Red

Dark Red

Bright Red

Dark
Red

Dark Red

Bright Red

Dark Red

Green

**Seasonable Stylish Hat - Block E
and
Poinsettia Hat Table Runner
Pattern**
Trace 2 in reverse

Poinsettia Table Runner
photo on page 9, pattern above
instructions on page 33

Seasonable Stylish Hats

photo on page 4
patterns on pages 19 - 29
poem by Sarah Haynes

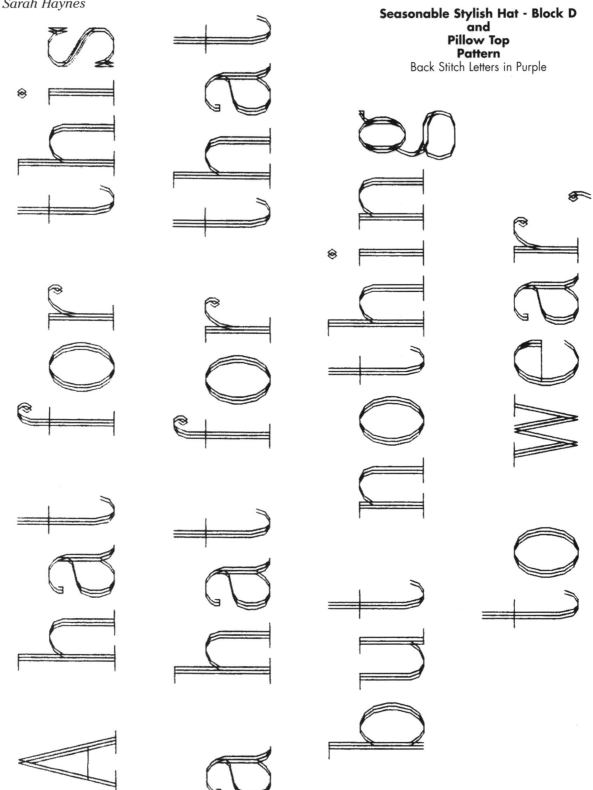

A hat for this
a hat for that
but nothing
to wear

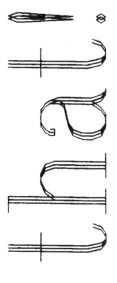

Finished Quilt Size - 36" x 36"

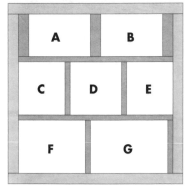

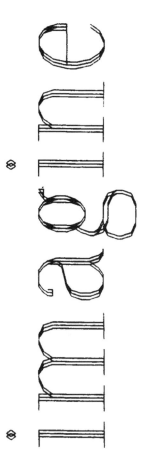

A hat for this
a hat for that
but nothing
to wear,
imagine that!

Seasonable Stylish Hats Pillow Top

photo on page 5
pattern at left

Seasonable Stylish Hats

photo on page 4

patterns on pages 19 - 29

Finished Quilt Size - 36" x 36"

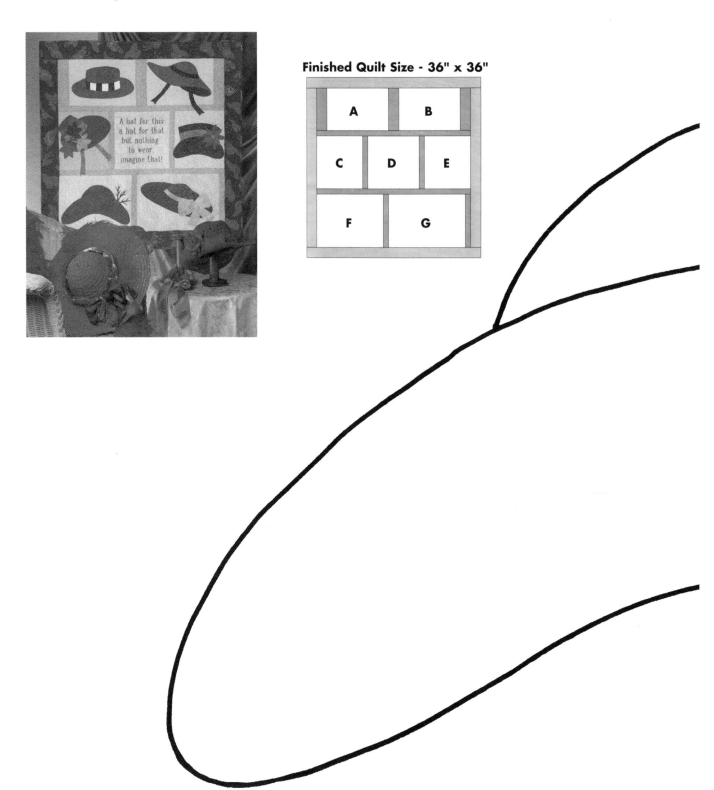

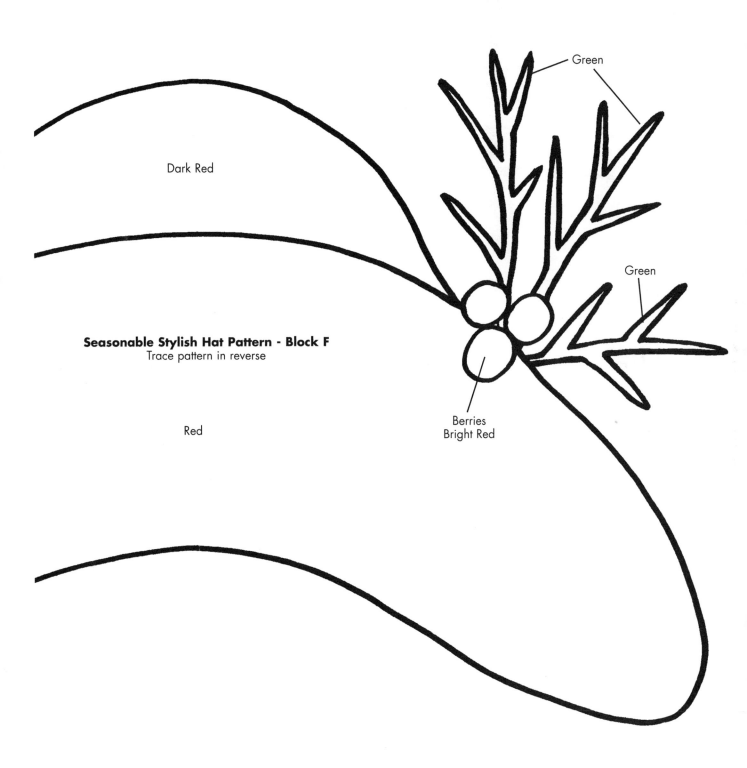

Green

Green

Dark Red

Seasonable Stylish Hat Pattern - Block F
Trace pattern in reverse

Red

Berries
Bright Red

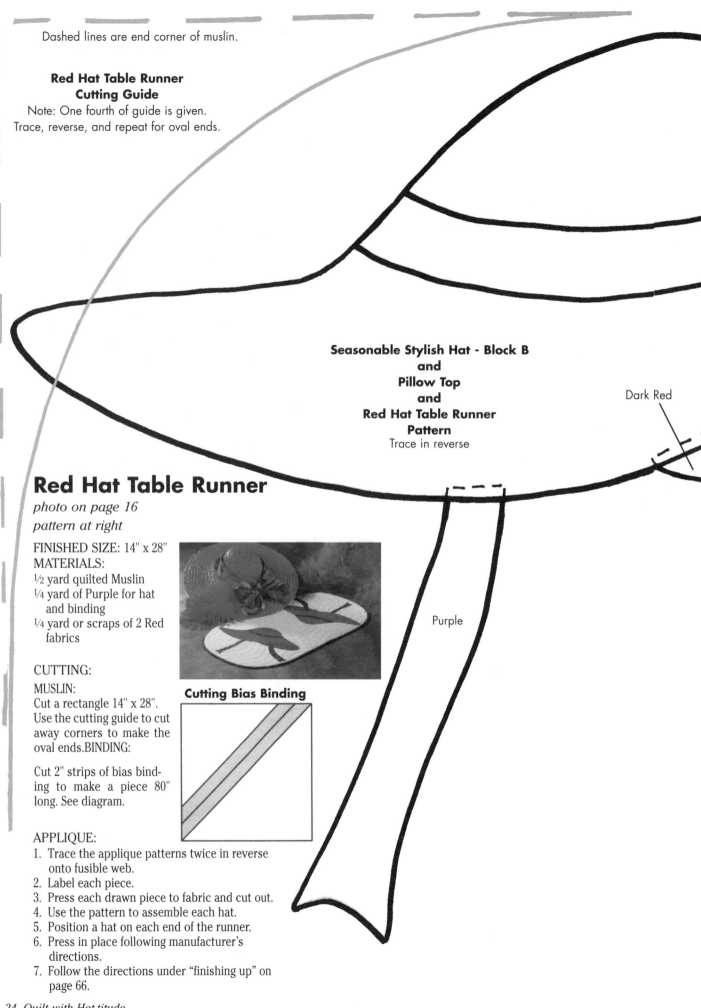

Dashed lines are end corner of muslin.

Red Hat Table Runner
Cutting Guide
Note: One fourth of guide is given.
Trace, reverse, and repeat for oval ends.

Seasonable Stylish Hat - Block B
and
Pillow Top
and
Red Hat Table Runner
Pattern
Trace in reverse

Dark Red

Purple

Red Hat Table Runner

photo on page 16
pattern at right

FINISHED SIZE: 14" x 28"
MATERIALS:
½ yard quilted Muslin
¼ yard of Purple for hat
   and binding
¼ yard or scraps of 2 Red
   fabrics

CUTTING:

MUSLIN:
Cut a rectangle 14" x 28".
Use the cutting guide to cut
away corners to make the
oval ends.BINDING:

Cut 2" strips of bias binding to make a piece 80"
long. See diagram.

Cutting Bias Binding

APPLIQUE:
1. Trace the applique patterns twice in reverse
   onto fusible web.
2. Label each piece.
3. Press each drawn piece to fabric and cut out.
4. Use the pattern to assemble each hat.
5. Position a hat on each end of the runner.
6. Press in place following manufacturer's
   directions.
7. Follow the directions under "finishing up" on
   page 66.

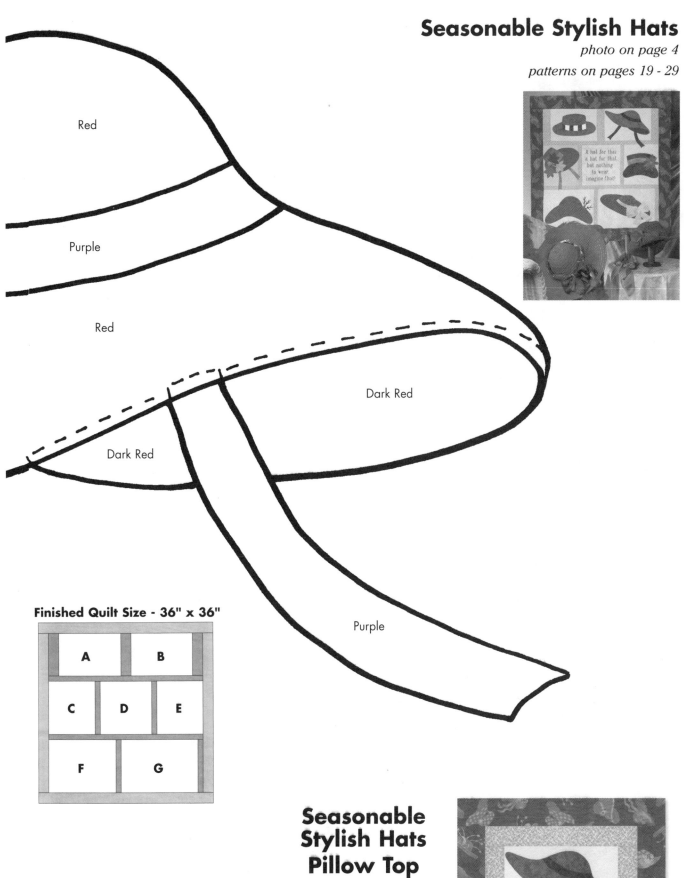

Seasonable Stylish Hats
photo on page 4
patterns on pages 19 - 29

Red

Purple

Red

Dark Red

Dark Red

Purple

Finished Quilt Size - 36" x 36"

A	B
C	D	E
F	G

Seasonable Stylish Hats Pillow Top
photo on page 5
pattern above

Seasonable Stylish Hats

photo on page 4

patterns on pages 19 - 29

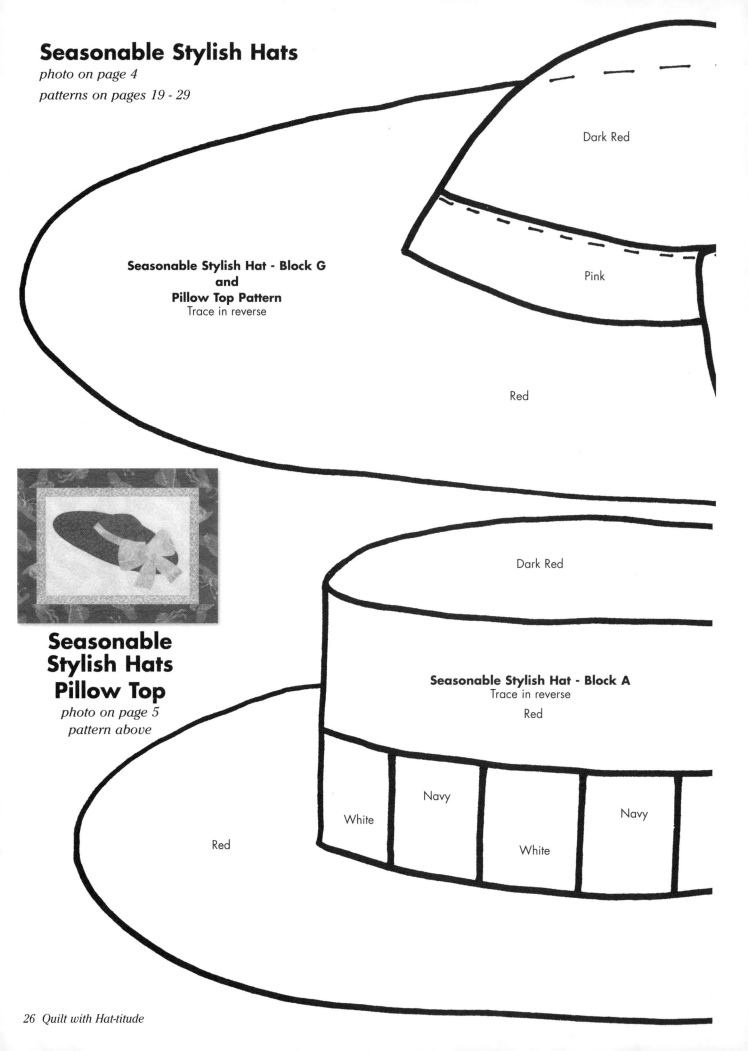

Dark Red

**Seasonable Stylish Hat - Block G
and
Pillow Top Pattern**
Trace in reverse

Pink

Red

Seasonable Stylish Hats Pillow Top

photo on page 5
pattern above

Dark Red

Seasonable Stylish Hat - Block A
Trace in reverse
Red

Navy

White

Navy

White

Red

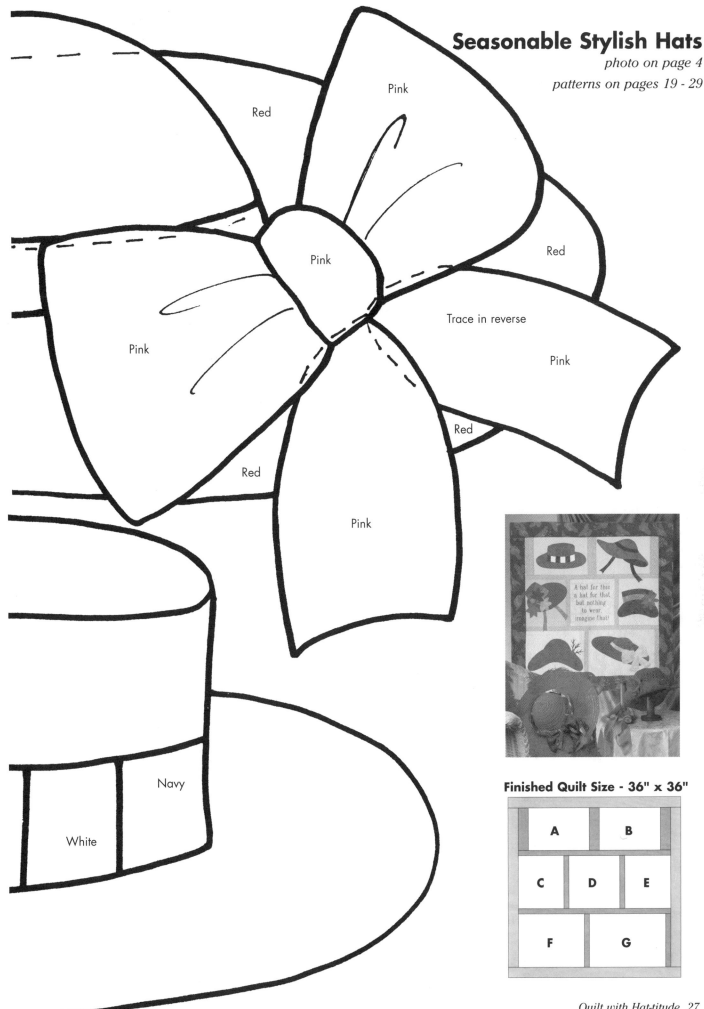

Seasonable Stylish Hats

photo on page 4
patterns on pages 19 - 29

Pink

Red

Pink

Pink

Red

Trace in reverse

Pink

Pink

Red

Red

Pink

Navy

White

Finished Quilt Size - 36" x 36"

A	B

C	D	E

F	G

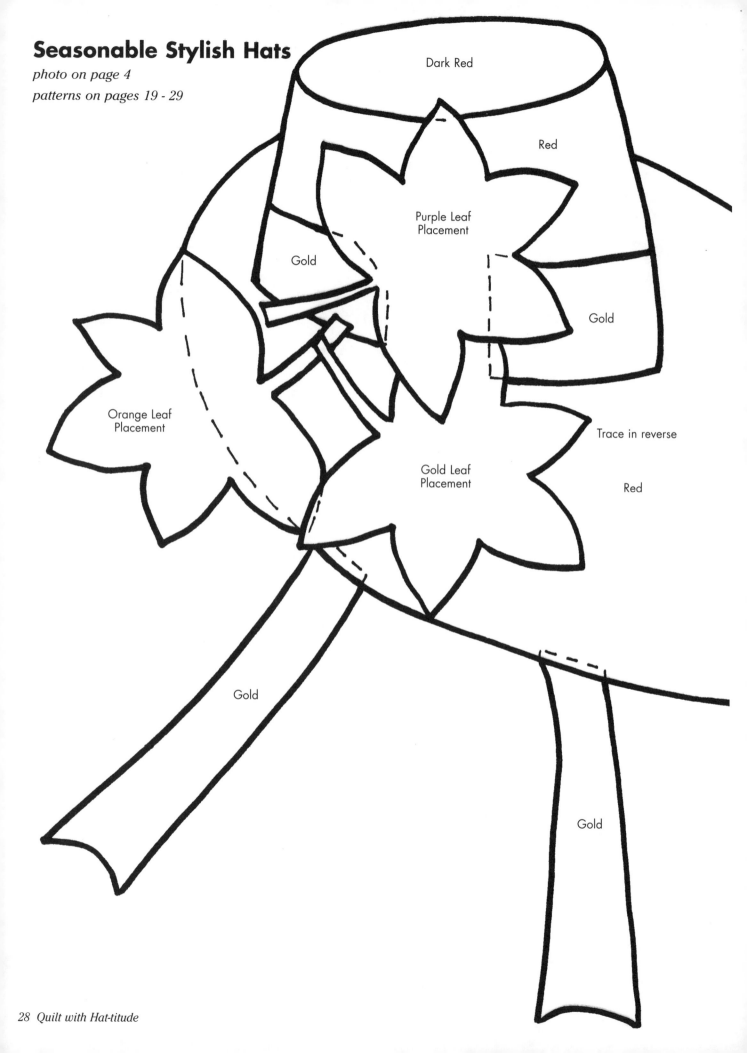

Seasonable Stylish Hats

photo on page 4
patterns on pages 19 - 29

Dark Red

Red

Purple Leaf
Placement

Gold

Gold

Orange Leaf
Placement

Trace in reverse

Red

Gold Leaf
Placement

Gold

Gold

Finished Quilt Size - 36" x 36"

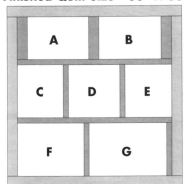

**Seasonable Stylish Hat -
Block C**

Red

**Seasonable Stylish Hat
Leaf Pattern**
Trace 3

All About Hat-titude™

Say, honest, girls, it's beastly
To wear a thing like that,
And make us tag like pups, behind
Your MERRY WIDOW HAT.

Copyright 1908
by L. Grollman

"Woman is the most superstitious animal beneath the moon. When a woman has a premonition that Tuesday will be a disaster, to which a man pays not heed, he will very likely lose his fortune then. This is not meant to be an occult vessel, and the universe drops its secrets into her far more quickly than it communicates them to the male."
~ Edward Dahlberg

"The future belongs to those who believe in the beauty of their dreams."
~ Eleanor Roosevelt

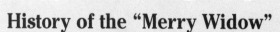

History of the "Merry Widow"

The Merry Widow is one of the most popular operettas of all time. Written by Franz Lehar, it opened in Europe on December 30, 1905. The show opened at The New Amsterdam theater in New York in 1907. Although considered risque for its time, The Merry Widow was an enormous succcess. It started a new dance craze, and its effects were even felt in the fashion industry. The popularity of this show sparked a brisk business in cocktails, corsets, and hats. These oversize, feather-laden hats featured wide brims, and became the rage before WWI.

"The special genius of women I believe to be electrical in movement, intuitive in function, spiritual in tendency." ~ Margaret Fuller

"Anyone who stops learning is old, whether at twenty or eighty. Anyone who keeps learning stays young. The greatest thing in life is to keep your mind young."
~ Margaret Fuller

"A little madness in the Spring is wholesome even for a Queen."
~ Emily Dickinson

"Grow old with me. the best is yet to be." ~ Robert Browning

Tea Pot Table Runner

photo on page 8

patterns on page 37

FINISHED SIZE: 14½" x 26½"

MATERIALS:

¼ yard Purple for border and binding

¼ yard or scraps of several Creme fabrics for background

¼ yard for applique: Chintz for tea pots; Gold Metallic for rim, handle and base

CUTTING:

Creme colored BACKGROUND:	Purple BORDERS:	
Cut two 9½" x 12½" end panels	Cut 2	1½" x 24½"
Cut eight 3½" squares	2	1½" x 14½"

BINDING:

Cut 2 strips of 2" x 44"

INSTRUCTIONS:

1. Lay out 8 Creme squares. 2 rows across, 4 squares each. See Block Layout diagram.
2. Sew together. Piece should measure 6½" x 12½". See diagram.
3. Add the background panels to each end.
4. Sew the 24½" side border strips to the piece.
5. Add the end border strips. Press.
6. Sew binding strips together.

APPLIQUE:

1. Trace the applique patterns twice in reverse onto fusible.
2. Label each piece.
3. Press each drawn piece to fabric.
4. Tea pot is chintz fabric. Rim, base and handle are Gold Metallic fabric.
5. Use the pattern to assemble each pot.
6. Position pieces on each end of the runner.
7. Press in place following your manufacturer's directions.
8. Follow the directions under "finishing up" on page 66.

Block Layout Diagram

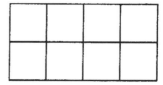

Turn as shown. Add background panel to to each end.

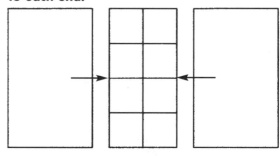

**Add side borders and end strips.
Add Applique designs.**

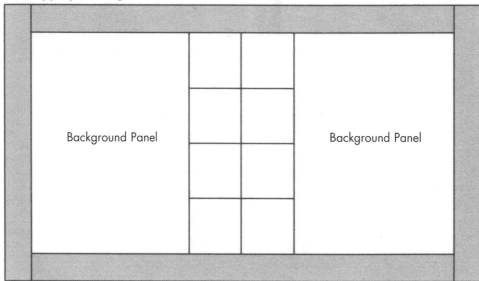

Background Panel   Background Panel

Poinsettia Table Runner

photo on page 9

patterns on page 19

FINISHED SIZE: 14½" x 28½"

MATERIALS:

¼ yard Red for border and binding
⅓ yard of Creme for background
½ yard of Backing fabric
¼ yard or scraps for applique: 2 shades of Red, Dark Red, Green
DMC Gold Pearl Cotton #5 for French Knots

CUTTING:

Creme colored BACKGROUND:
Cut one 10½" x 24½"

Red BORDERS:
Cut 2   2½" x 24½"
    2   2½" x 14½"
    4   2½" squares

BINDING:
Cut 2 strips of 2" x 44"

Diagram 1

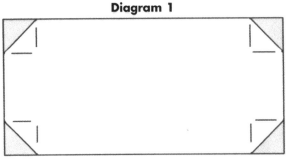

INSTRUCTIONS:

1. With right sides together, sew a 2½" Red square to each corner of the Creme background. See diagram 1.
2. Fold each square back and press the seam open.
3. Cut off excess in back if desired.
4. Sew the 24½" side border strips to each side.
5. Sew the 14½" end border strips to each end. Press.
6. Measure 2½" from each of the 4 corners. See diagram 2.
7. Mark the line with a pencil and cut off the corners.
8. Sew binding strips together to measure 70".

Diagram 2

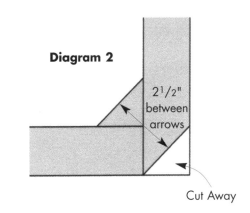

2½" between arrows

Cut Away

APPLIQUE:

1. Trace the applique patterns twice in reverse, onto fusible web.
2. Label each piece.
3. Press each drawn piece to fabric and cut out.
4. Use the pattern to assemble each hat.
5. Position a hat on each end of the runner.
6. Press in place following manufacturer's directions.
7. Follow the directions under "finishing up" on page 66.

Add side border strips. Press. Add end border strips.

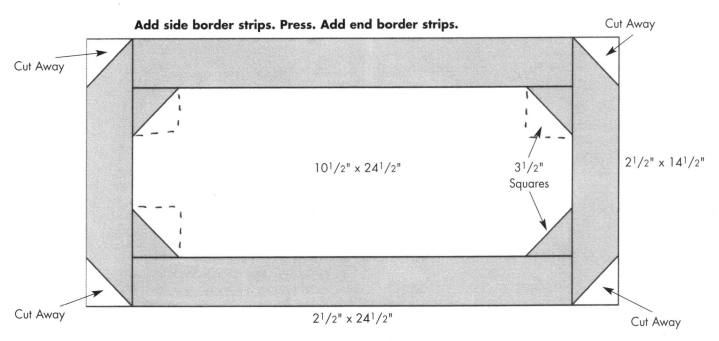

Cut Away

Cut Away

Cut Away

Cut Away

Cut Away

10½" x 24½"

3½" Squares

2½" x 14½"

2½" x 24½"

Tea Party Wall Quilt

photo on page 7
patterns on pages 36 - 41
poem by Sarah Haynes

FINISHED SIZE: 34" x 34"
MATERIALS:
½ yard for outer border and binding
¼ yard of Purple for inner border (we used checkered fabric)
¼ yard of medium Purple for sashing
1 Fat Quarter of Creme for center block
½ yard of Creme fabric for all other blocks
1 yard of backing fabric
For applique, ¼ yard cuts (or scraps) of 2 shades of Red, 3 shades of Pink/Purple chintz, 3 shades of Pink, 3 shades of Purple/Violet, 2 shades of Green, White, Metallic gold • *DMC* Red Pearl Cotton #5 • Steam-A-Seam II fusible web • Baby size *Warm & Natural* Cotton Batting • Disappearing pen

CUTTING:

Cut out BLOCKS from Creme
1	9½" x 10½"	for center Block E
4	9" squares	for A, C, G, and I
2	7½" x 8"	for B and H
2	6½" x 7½"	for D and F

Cut out from INNER BORDER fabric
2 strips   1½" x 28½" for sides
2 strips   1½" x 30½" for top and bottom

Cut out from OUTER BORDER fabric
2 strips   2¼" x 30½" for sides
2 strips   2¼" x 34" for top and bottom

Cut out for SASHING from Purple
4	1½" x 9"	for A, C, G, and I
2	1½" x 9½"	for E
2	1½" x 28½"	between rows 1-2, and 2-3.

Cut out SASHING from Tan
4	1½" x 7½"	for sides of D and F
4	1½" x 8"	for sides of B and H
4	1½" x 8½"	for top and bottom of D and F
2	1½" x 9½"	for bottom of B and top of H

BINDING:

Cut 2" strips and sew together for 140"

INSTRUCTIONS:

1. Cut out all the blocks, sashing and border strips.
2. Trace the poem on Block E (9½" x 10½") with a disappearing pen.
3. Back Stitch the words using Red Pearl Cotton. Press.
4. Arrange blocks as shown in the Block Arrangement Diagram.
5. Sew in rows across, with right sides together, pressing each seam as you go. See the Diagrams for Borders/ Sashing and Assembly .
6. **Row 1**: Sew a 1½" x 8" Tan strip to each side of the 7½" x 8" center Block B.
7. Sew a 1½" x 9½" Tan strip to the bottom of Block B.
8. Sew a 1½" x 9" Purple strip to the right side of Block A.
9. Sew a 1½" x 9" Purple strip to the left side of Block C.
10. Sew Block A to B, then to Block C.
11. Sew a 1½" x 28½" Purple sashing strip across the bottom of Row 1.
12. **Row 2**: Sew a 1½" x 9½" Purple sashing strip to each side of the center Block E.
13. Sew a 1½" x 7½" Tan strip to both sides of Blocks D and F.
14. Sew a 1½" x 8½" Tan strip to the top and bottom of Blocks D and F.
15. Sew Block D to Block E, then to Block F.
16. Sew a 1½" x 28½" Purple sashing strip across the bottom of Row 2.

17. **Row 3**: Sew a 1½" x 8" Tan strip to each side of the 7½" x 8" center Block H.
18. Sew a 1½" x 9½" Tan strip to the top.
19. Sew a 1½" x 9" Purple strip to the right side of Block G.
20. Sew a 1½" x 9" Purple strip to the left side of Block I.
21. Sew Block G to H, then to Block I.
22. Sew Row 2 to the bottom of Row 1.
    Sew Row 3 to the bottom of Row 2.
23. Sew the 1½" x 28½" inner borders to each side. Press. Sew the 1½" x 30½" inner borders to the top & bottom.
24. Sew the 2¼" x 30½" borders to each side. Press. Sew the 2¼" x 34" borders to the top & bottom.

APPLIQUE:

Tea pots and cups can be made from a solid fabric with little or no embellishment by tracing the outline of the entire design.
To use several fabrics that co-ordinate, trace each piece of the design separately.

1. Trace each applique pattern in reverse onto fusible web. Label each piece.
2. Press each drawn piece to fabric and cut out.
3. Use the pattern to assemble each applique.
4. Lay out the applique on each block and center as needed.
5. Press in place following manufacturer's directions.
6. Follow the directions under "finishing up" on page 66.

Tea Party Wall Quilt

photo on page 7
patterns on pages 36 - 41

Block Arrangement Diagram

Quilt Assembly Diagram

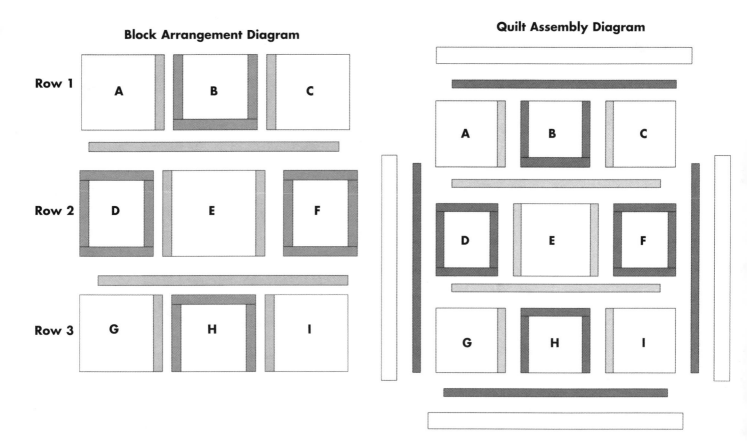

Assembly Borders/Sashing Diagram

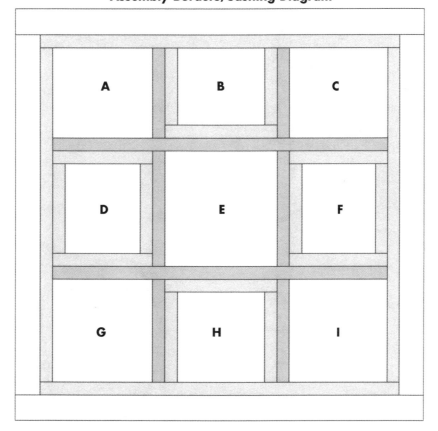

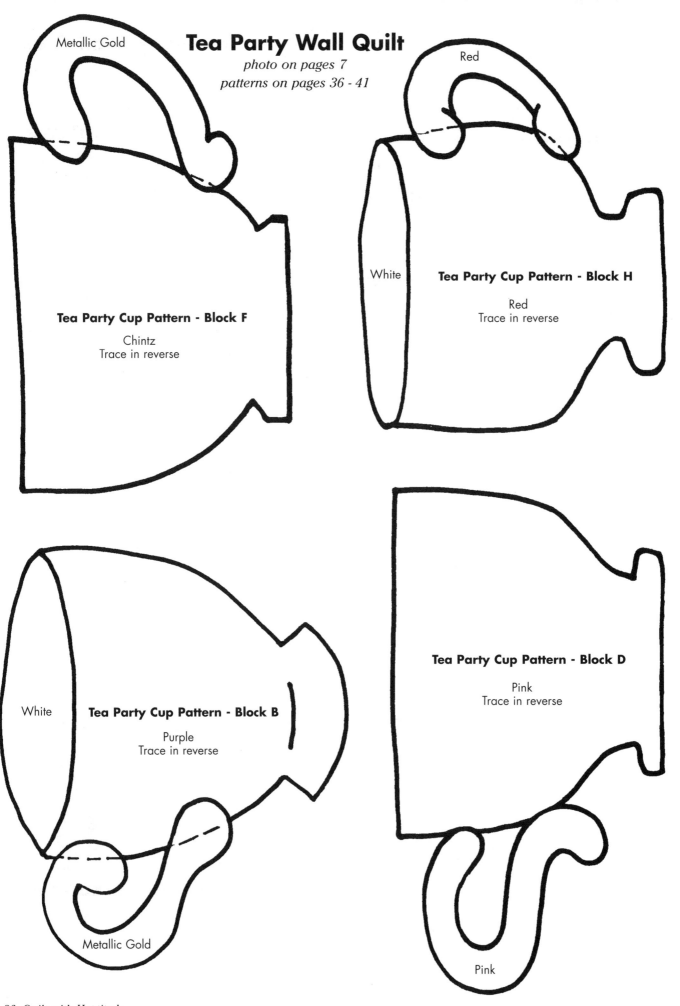

Tea Party Wall Quilt

photo on pages 7
patterns on pages 36 - 41

Metallic Gold

Red

Tea Party Cup Pattern - Block F

Chintz
Trace in reverse

White

Tea Party Cup Pattern - Block H

Red
Trace in reverse

White

Tea Party Cup Pattern - Block B

Purple
Trace in reverse

Metallic Gold

Tea Party Cup Pattern - Block D

Pink
Trace in reverse

Pink

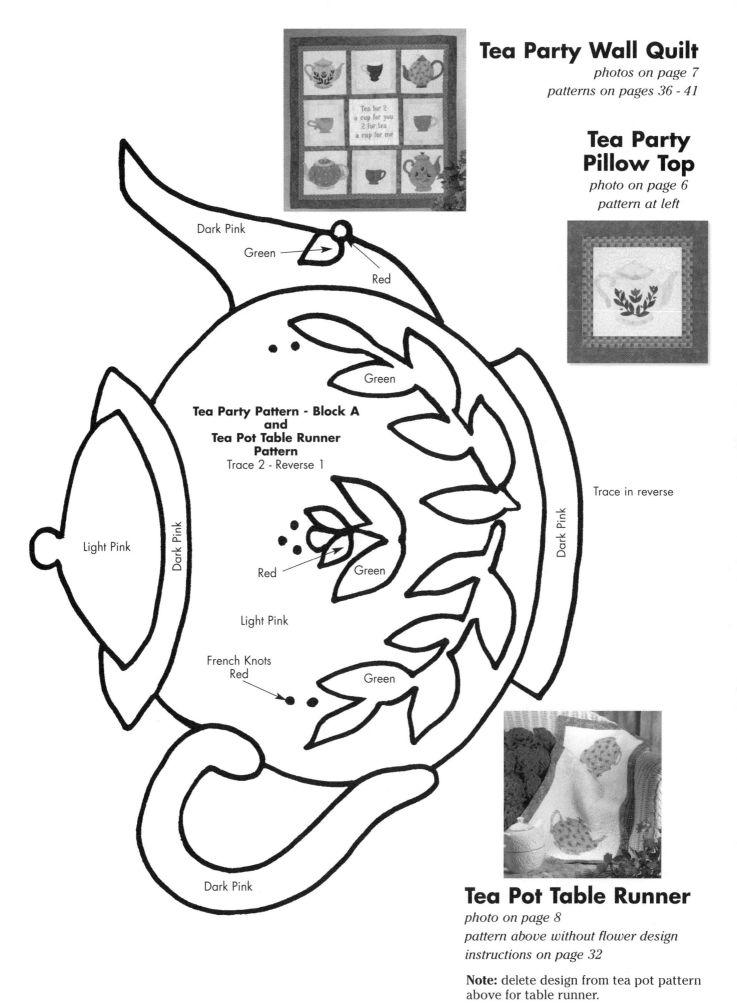

Tea Party Wall Quilt

photos on page 7
patterns on pages 36 - 41

Tea Party
Pillow Top

photo on page 6
pattern at left

Dark Pink

Green

Red

Green

Tea Party Pattern - Block A
and
Tea Pot Table Runner
Pattern
Trace 2 - Reverse 1

Trace in reverse

Light Pink

Dark Pink

Dark Pink

Red

Green

Light Pink

French Knots
Red

Green

Dark Pink

Tea Pot Table Runner

photo on page 8
pattern above without flower design
instructions on page 32

Note: delete design from tea pot pattern
above for table runner.

Tea Party Wall Quilt

photo on pages 6 - 7
patterns on pages 36 - 41

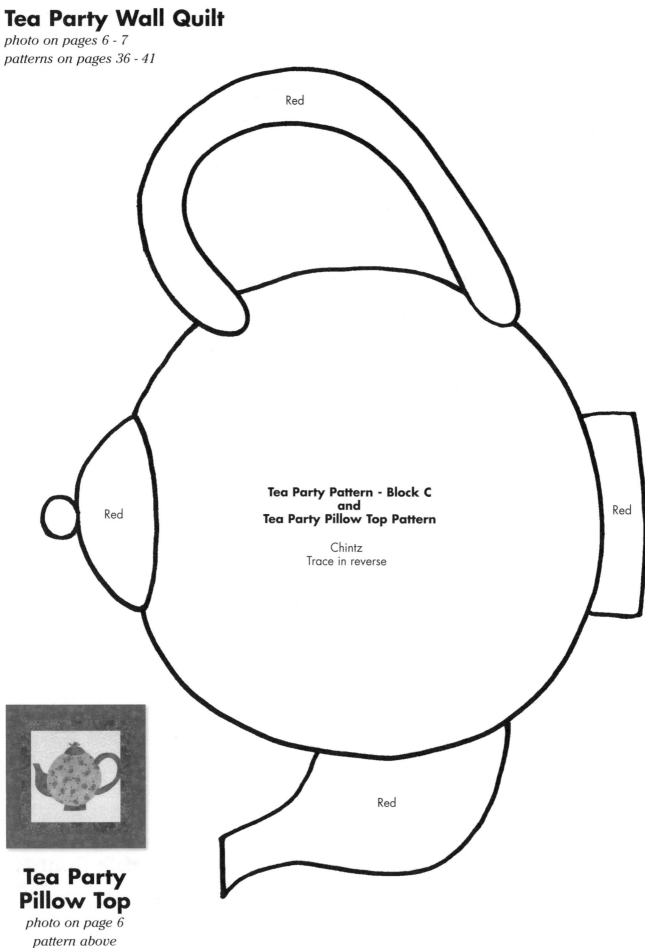

Red

Red

Red

**Tea Party Pattern - Block C
and
Tea Party Pillow Top Pattern**

Chintz
Trace in reverse

Red

Red

Tea Party
Pillow Top

photo on page 6
pattern above

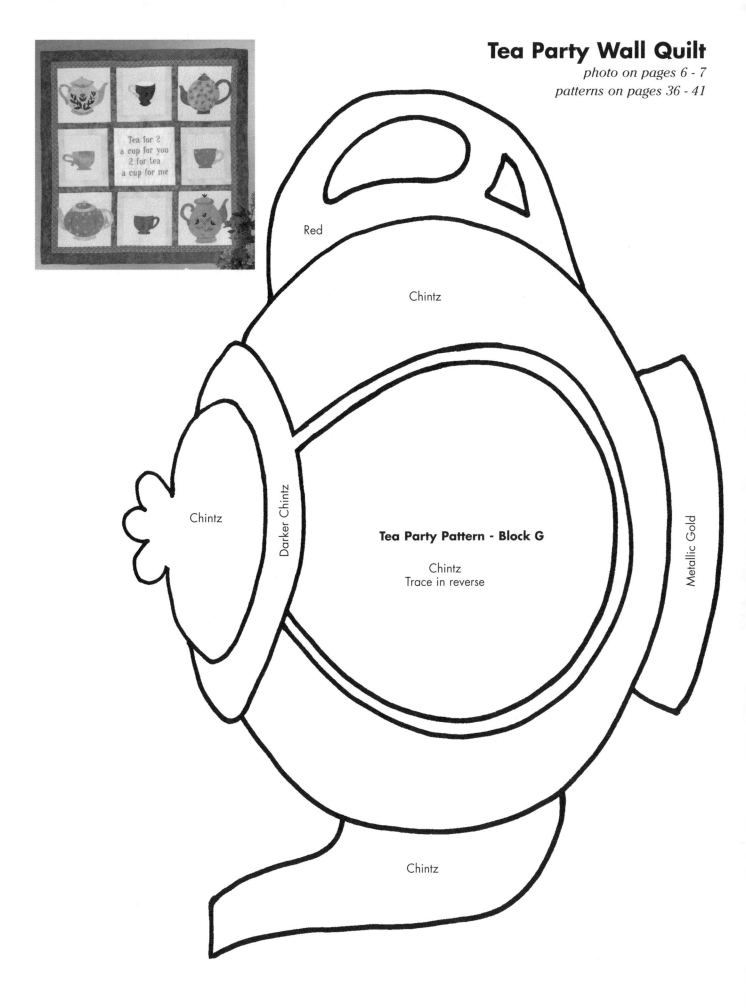

Tea Party Wall Quilt

photo on pages 6 - 7
patterns on pages 36 - 41

Tea for 2
a cup for you
2 for tea
a cup for me

Red

Chintz

Chintz

Darker Chintz

Tea Party Pattern - Block G

Chintz
Trace in reverse

Metallic Gold

Chintz

Tea Party Wall Quilt

photo on page 7
patterns on pages
poem by Sarah Hayes

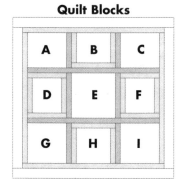

Quilt Blocks

A	B	C
D	E	F
G	H	I

**Tea Party Pattern -
Block E**

Tea for 2
a cup for you
2 for tea
a cup for me

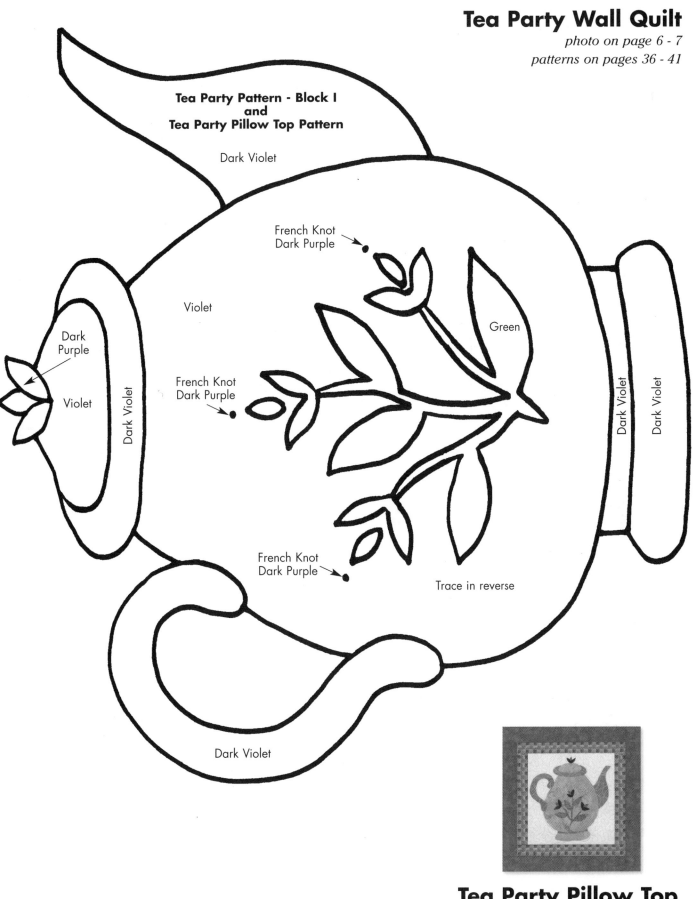

Tea Party Pattern - Block I
and
Tea Party Pillow Top Pattern

Dark Violet

French Knot
Dark Purple

Violet

Dark
Purple

Violet

Dark Violet

French Knot
Dark Purple

Green

Dark Violet

Dark Violet

French Knot
Dark Purple

Trace in reverse

Dark Violet

Tea Party Pillow Top

photo on page 6
pattern above

Garden Club Wall Quilt

photo on page 11

patterns on pages 43 - 51

FINISHED SIZE: 30" x 38"

MATERIALS:
½ yard for border and binding
4 fat quarters of Creme for blocks and sashing
4 fat quarters of Light Green for blocks and sashing
1¼ yards of backing fabric
⅓ yard of Purple for sashing & inner border

¼ yard cuts (or scraps) of 2 shades of Red for flowers and hat, 3 shades of Green leaves, 2 shades of Tan for the hat, 4 shades of Purple for gloves and flowers, Gray and Brown for garden tools, Metallic Gold for the watering can • 3 Gold 1⅛" buttons • 2 Red 1" buttons • Steam-A-Seam II fusible web • *Warm & Natural* Cotton Batting

CUTTING:

Cut out BLOCKS from Creme or Light Green

A	10½" x 12½"	D	7½" x 9½"
B	12½" x 13½"	E	8½" x 15½"
C	7½" x 13½"	F	6½" x 8½"

Cut out Purple INNER BORDER
2 strips   1½" x 26½" for top and bottom
2 strips   1½" x 32½" for sides

Cut out Green OUTER BORDER
2 strips   2½" x 34½" for sides
2 strips   2½" x 30½" for top and bottom

Cut out Purple SASHING
2   1½" x 24½" goes between rows
1   1½" x 12½" goes between Blocks A and B

Cut out Green SASHING
1   1½" x 13½" for Block C top
1   2½" x 13½" for Block C bottom
1   1½" x 8½" for Block F

Cut out Creme SASHING
2   2½" x 9½" for Block D side
1   1½" x 11½" for Block D bottom
2   1½" x 8½" for Block E

BINDING:
Cut 2" strips and sew together for 140"

INSTRUCTIONS:
1. Cut out all the blocks, sashing and border strips.
2. Arrange the blocks as shown on the Assembly Diagram.
3. Sew in rows across, with right sides together, pressing each seam as you go. See Borders/Sashing Diagram.
4. **Row 1**: Sew Block A to the left side of the 2½" x 12½" Purple strip.
5. Sew Block B to the right side of the Purple strip.
6. Sew one 1½" x 24½" strip to the bottom of Row 1.
7. **Row 2**: Sew a 1½" x 13½" Green strip to the top of Block C.
8. Sew the 2½" x 13½" Green strip to the bottom of Block C.
9. Sew a 2½" x 9½" Creme strip to each side of Block D.
10. Sew a 1½" x 11½" Creme strip to the bottom of Block D.
11. Sew Block C to the left side of Block D.
12. Sew the other 1½" x 24½" strip across the bottom of Row 2.
13. **Row 3**: Sew a 1½" x 8½" Creme strip to each side of Block E.
14. Sew a 1½" x 8½" Green strip to the right side of Block F.
15. Sew Block E to the left side of Block F.
16. Sew Row 2 to the bottom of Row 1 and sew Row 3 to the bottom of Row 2.
17. Sew the 1½" x 32½" Purple inner border strips to both sides.
18. Sew the 1½" x 26½" Purple inner border strips to the top and bottom.
19. Sew the 2½" x 34½" outer border strips to the sides.
20. Sew the 2½" x 30½" border strips to the top & bottom.

Quilt Assembly Diagram

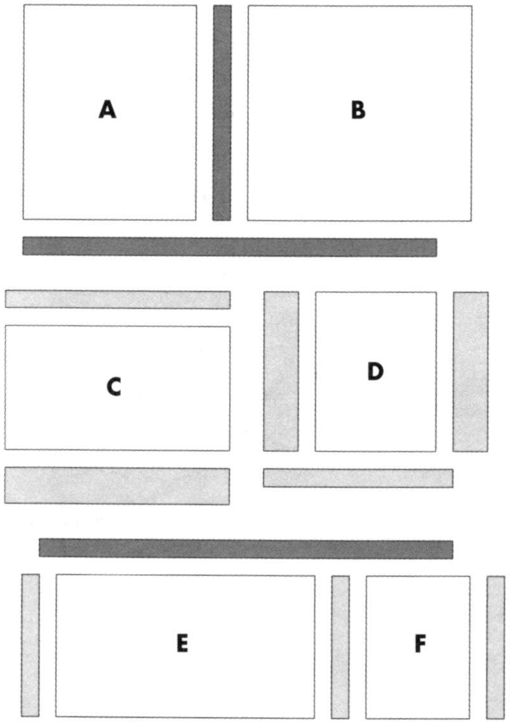

APPLIQUE:
1. Trace the applique patterns in reverse onto fusible web. Label each piece.
2. Press each drawn piece to fabric and cut out.
3. Use the pattern to assemble each block.
4. Lay out the designs on each block and center as needed.
5. Press in place following manufacturer's directions.
6. Follow the directions under "finishing up" on page 66.
7. Bows: Press a 1½" x 15" strip of fusible web along one side of a 3" x 16" strip of Purple fabric.
8. Peel off the paper backing and fold the fabric in half lengthways.
9. Press together and cut away the edges that are not stuck together.
10. Cut two ½" strips 15" long. Tie two bows and hand stitch to each garden glove.

Garden Club Wall Quilt

photo on page 11
patterns on pages 43 - 51

Borders/Sashing Diagram

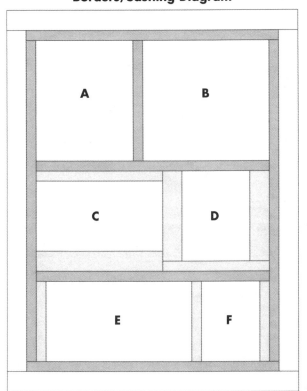

Garden Club Pillow Top

photo on page 11
patterns on page 43 - 51

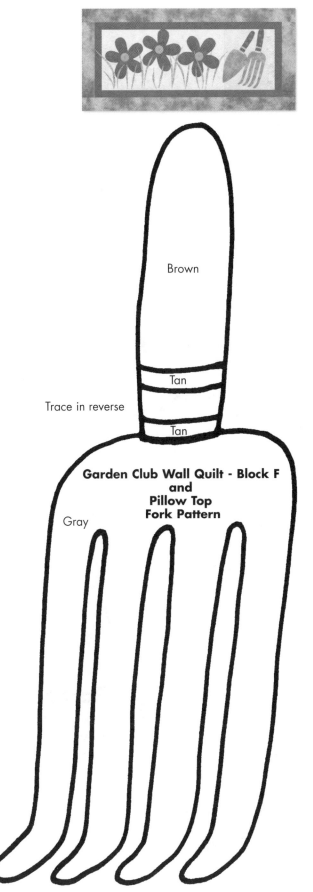

Brown

Tan

Trace in reverse

Tan

**Garden Club Wall Quilt - Block F
and
Pillow Top
Fork Pattern**

Gray

Garden Club Wall Quilt

photo on page 11
patterns on pages 43 - 51

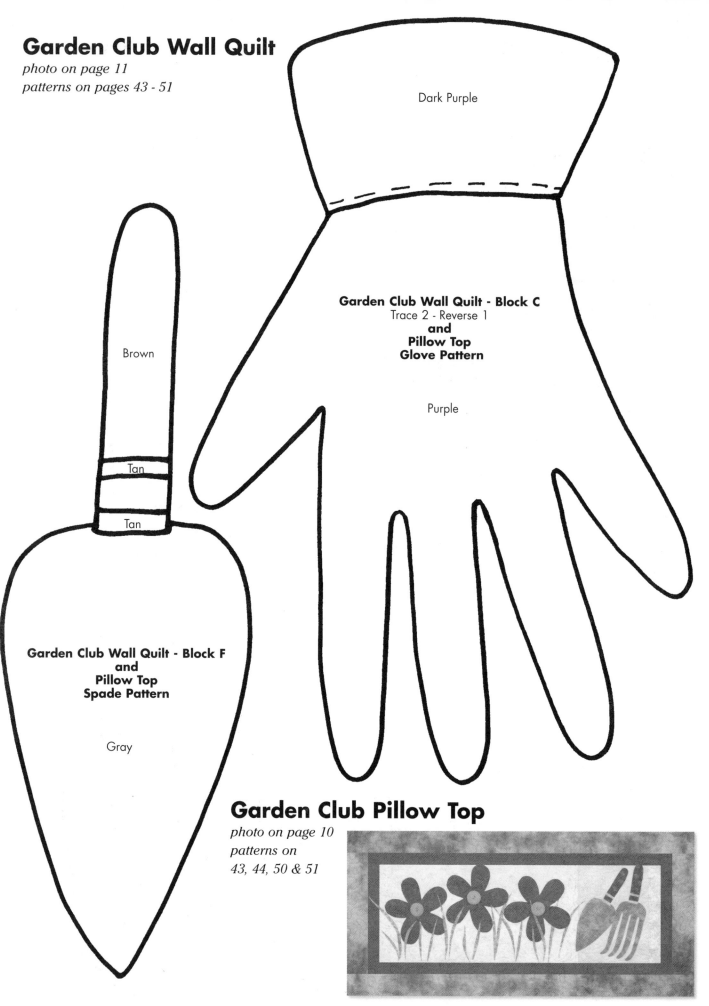

Dark Purple

Brown

Garden Club Wall Quilt - Block C
Trace 2 - Reverse 1
and
Pillow Top
Glove Pattern

Purple

Tan

Tan

Garden Club Wall Quilt - Block F
and
Pillow Top
Spade Pattern

Gray

Garden Club Pillow Top

photo on page 10
patterns on
43, 44, 50 & 51

Garden Club Wall Quilt

photo on page 11
patterns on pages 43 - 51

Purple

Red Button →

Purple

Red Button →

Garden Club Wall Quilt - Block D
and
Pillow Top
Pattern

Trace in reverse

Green
Stems and
Leaves

Garden Club
Pillow Top

photo on page 9
pattern above

Garden Club Wall Quilt

photo on page 11
patterns on pages 43 - 51

Quilt Block Diagram

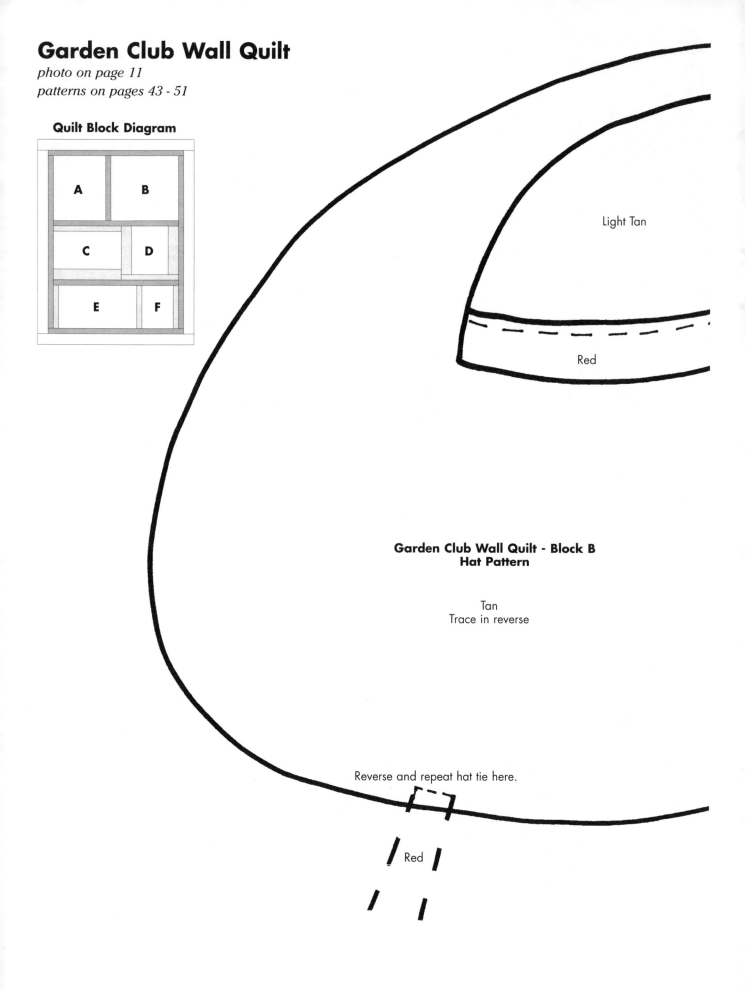

Light Tan

Red

Garden Club Wall Quilt - Block B
Hat Pattern

Tan
Trace in reverse

Reverse and repeat hat tie here.

Red

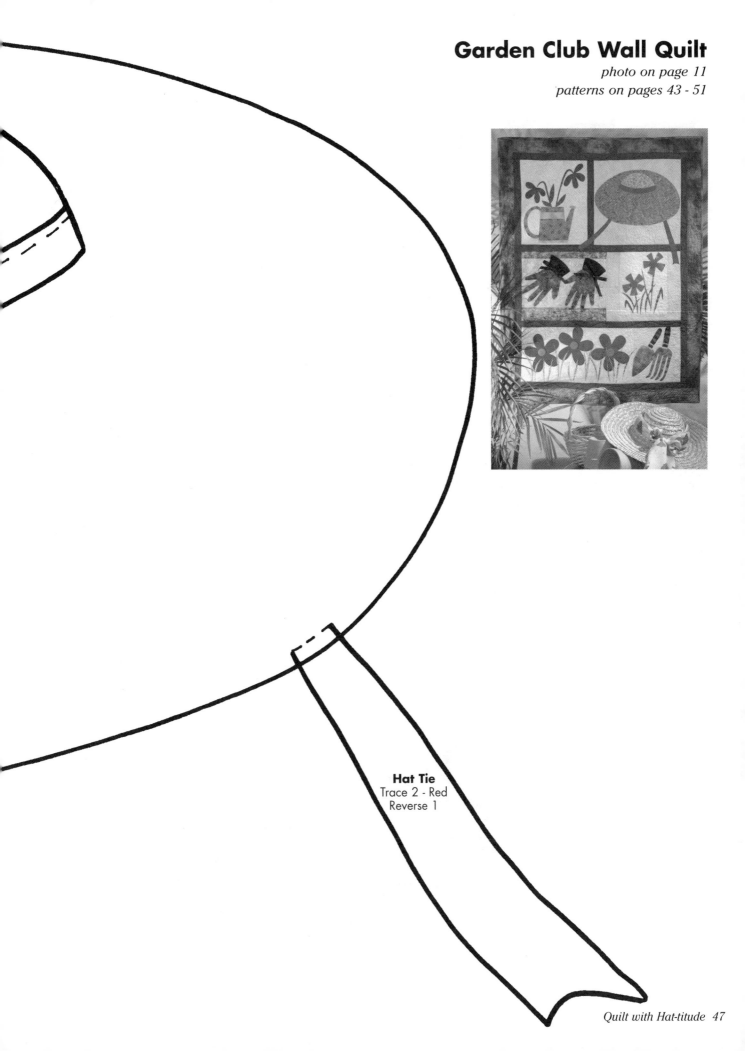

Hat Tie
Trace 2 - Red
Reverse 1

Garden Club Wall Quilt

photo on page 11
patterns on pages 43 - 51

Purple

Watering Can Pillow Top

photo on page 10
pattern at right

Watering Can Table Runner

photo on page 67
pattern at right - Color choices for pattern pieces on page 66 diagram

Quilt Block Diagram

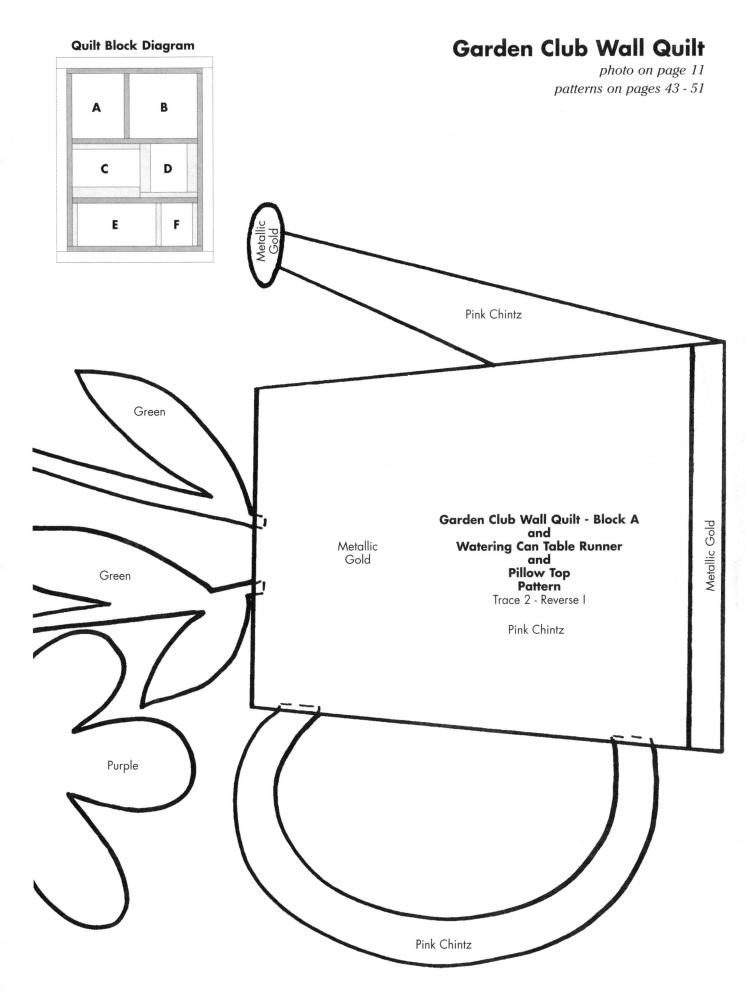

A	B

C	D

E	F

Garden Club Wall Quilt

photo on page 11
patterns on pages 43 - 51

Metallic Gold

Pink Chintz

Green

Green

Purple

Metallic Gold

**Garden Club Wall Quilt - Block A
and
Watering Can Table Runner
and
Pillow Top
Pattern**
Trace 2 - Reverse I

Pink Chintz

Metallic Gold

Pink Chintz

Garden Club Wall Quilt

photo on page 11
patterns on pages 43 - 51

Optional: Orange
Flower Center
instead of buttons
for Table Runner
Cut 3

**Garden Club
Wall Quilt - Block A
and
Pillow Top Pattern**

Red

Red

Optional: Orange Flower
Center

Orange Button

Leave flows over into border here.

Trace in reverse

Green Grass

Garden Club Pillow Top

photo on page 10
patterns on
43, 44, 50 & 51

Orange Button

Red

Orange Button

Flower
Table Runner

photo on page 13

patterns on page 45

FINISHED SIZE: 16½" x 24½"

MATERIALS:
½ yard Green for border, backing
and binding
⅓ yard of Creme for background
¼ yard or scraps for applique: Pink, Red,
and Green

CUTTING:
Creme colored BACKGROUND:
Cut one 12½" x 20½" OR
Cut 2   7½" x 12½" and
        1   6½" x 12½"

Green BORDERS:
Cut 2   2½" x 20½"
        2   2½" x 16½"

BINDING:
Cut 2 strips of 2" x 44"

INSTRUCTIONS:
1. If you used 1 piece for the background, proceed to step 2.
   Sew pieces of background together. See diagram below.
2. Sew the 20½" side border strips to each side. Press.
3. Sew the 16½" end border strips to each end. Press.
4. Sew strips together end to end to measure 88" for binding.

APPLIQUE:
1. Trace the applique patterns in reverse onto fusible web.
2. Label each piece.
3. Press each drawn piece to fabric and cut out.
4. Flowers are Pink with Red centers. Stems and leaves are Green.
5. Use the pattern to position pieces on each end of the runner.
6. Press in place following manufacturer's directions.
7. Follow the directions under "finishing up" on page 66.

Use flower and stem/grass patterns page 45 to make up quilt motif shown in table runner photo.

Flower Table Runner Assembly

Friends and Flowers Wall Hanging

photo on page 12
patterns on pages 54 - 55
poem by Sarah Haynes

FINISHED SIZE: 13" x 20"
MATERIALS:
½ yard Green for border and backing
Fat quarter of Creme or Muslin for background
Scraps for applique: Purple for flowers, Green for leaves
DMC Green Pearl Cotton #5 for poem
Warm & Natural Cotton Batting
2 Red ⅞" Buttons • Red thread

CUTTING:
Creme BACKGROUND
Cut one 9½" x 16½"

Green BORDERS
2   2¼" x 20" for top and bottom
2   2¼" x 9½" for sides

INSTRUCTIONS:
1. Trace the poem on the 9½" x 16½" rectangle.
2. Back Stitch the words using Green Pearl Cotton. Press.
3. Sew the 2¼" x 9½" border strips to each side. See Assembly diagram.
4. Sew the 2¼" x 20" border strips to the top and bottom. Press.

APPLIQUE:
1. Trace the applique patterns in reverse onto fusible web.
2. Label each piece.
3. Press each drawn piece to fabric.
4. Cut out and position a stem and flower on each side of the poem.
5. Press in place, following manufacturer's directions.
6. Position the pieced top face down on the backing fabric.
7. Place these two on top of a single layer of cotton batting. See diagram.
8. Sew a ¼" seam all around, leaving about 6" open for turning.
9. Trim the excess and turn right side out.
10. Push out the corners and hand-stitch the opening closed.
11. Hand-stitch dowel rod across the top of the back for hanging.

Quilt Border Assembly

Place pieced top face down on the backing fabric. Place these two on top of a single layer of cotton batting.

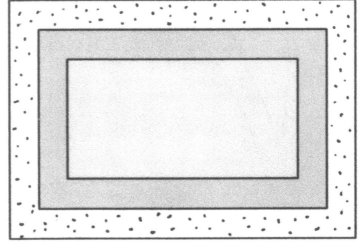

Friends and Flowers Wall Hanging

photo on page 12
patterns below
poem by Sarah Haynes

Purple

Trace in reverse

Back Stitch letters in Green

You can pick

you can pick

but don

your friend

Green

Friends and Flowers Wall Hanging

photo on page 12
patterns below
poem by Sarah Haynes

your friends

your flowers

1't pick

1's flowers

A Lady's Sampler

photo on page 15
patterns on pages 58 - 63

FINISHED SIZE: 27" x 28"

MATERIALS:
½ yard Red for border and binding
4 fat quarters Creme/Ecru for blocks
4 fat quarters Purple for blocks
¼ yard Pink for sashing
1 yard backing fabric
¼ yard cuts or scraps for applique: 5 shades Light to Dark Red (hat, purse & candy box), 3 shades Purple (glove, shoe & hat band), 3 shades Pink (shoe & tea pot), 2 shades Brown (candies), Creme (candy box), White (glove & cuffs), Metallic Gold (buckle, cuff links & tea pot handle)
DMC White Pearl Cotton #5 • Steam-A-Seam II fusible web • *Warm & Natural* Cotton Batting

CUTTING:
Cut BLOCKS
A   6½" x 7½" Purple
B   7½" x 7½" Creme
C   7½" x 8½" Creme
D   6½" x 14½" Creme
E   4½" x 5½" Dark Purple
F   4½" x 5½" Creme
G   9½" x 9½" Purple
H   6½" x 13½" Purple

Cut SASHING from pink
1   1½" x 7½" for "a"
1   2½" x 7½" for "b"
1   1½" x 24½" for "c"
3   1½" x 6½" for "d", "j" and "k"
1   1½" x 9½" for "e"
1   1½" x 10½" for "f"
2   1½" x 5½" for "g" and "h"
2   1½" x 15½" for "i" and "l"

Cut from OUTER BORDER fabric
2 strips   2½" x 27½"
2 strips   2½" x 24½"

BINDING
Cut 2" strips to make 115"

HAT BOW:
Cut a 3" x 24" strip of Purple fabric

INSTRUCTIONS:
1. Cut out all the blocks and border strips.
2. Arrange blocks as shown on Assembly Diagram.
3. Sew in sections, with right sides together, pressing each seam as you go. See Section Layout and Construction Diagrams.
4. **Section 1**: Sew Sashing "a" to the top of Block B, sashing "b" to the bottom of Block B.
5. Sew Block A to the top, and Block C to the bottom of Block B.
6. Sew sashing "c" to the right side of Section 1.
7. **Section 2**: Sew sashing "d" to the right side of Block D.
8. **Section 3**: Sew sashings "g" and "h" to the top and bottom of Block E.
9. Sew Block F to the bottom of Block E.
10. Sew sashing "f" to the left side of Block E-F.
11. Sew sashing "e" to the top of Block G.
12. Sew Block G to the left side of sashing "f".
13. **Section 4**: Sew the sashing "j" and "k" to each side of Block H.
14. Sew sashing "i" to the top, and "l" to the bottom of Block H.
15. Sew Sections 2, 3 and 4 together.
16. Sew Section 1 to the left side.
17. Sew the 2½" x 24½" borders to each side. Press. Sew the 2½" x 27½" borders to the top and bottom.

APPLIQUE:
1. Trace the applique patterns in reverse onto fusible web. Label each piece.
2. Press each drawn piece to fabric and cut out.
3. The small glove on Block H has White Pearl Cotton stitched details and French Knots.
4. Use the pattern to assemble each applique.
5. Lay out the designs on the blocks.
6. Press in place following manufacturer's directions.
7. Hat Bow: Press a 1½" x 24" strip of fusible web along one side of a 3" x 24" strip of Purple fabric.
8. Peel off the paper backing and fold the fabric in half lengthways.
9. Press together and cut away the edges that are not stuck together.
10. Cut a 1" x 24" strip. Tie the bow and hand-stitch to the hat.
11. Follow the directions under "finishing up" on page 66.

A Lady's Sampler

photo on page 15
patterns on pages 58 - 63

Section Layout

Section 1

A

a

B

b

C

c

Section 2

D

d

Section 3

e

G

f

g

E

h

F

Section 4

i

j

H

k

l

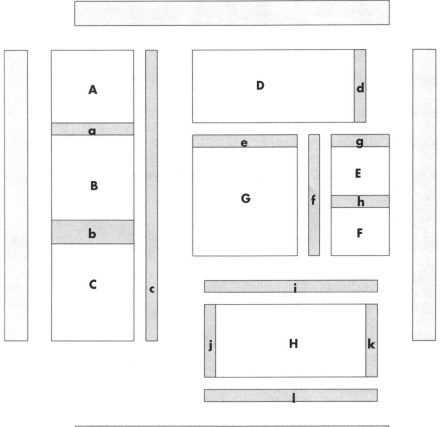

Adding Borders

A

a

B

b

C

c

D

d

e

G

f

g

E

h

F

i

j

H

k

l

A Lady's Sampler

photo on page 15
patterns on pages 58 - 63

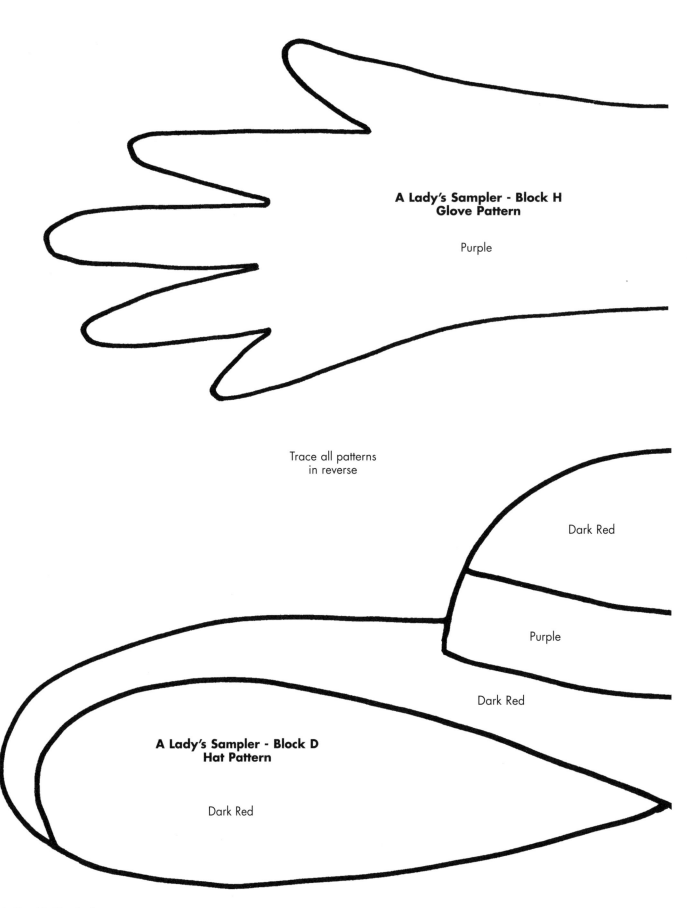

**A Lady's Sampler - Block H
Glove Pattern**

Purple

Trace all patterns
in reverse

Dark Red

Purple

Dark Red

**A Lady's Sampler - Block D
Hat Pattern**

Dark Red

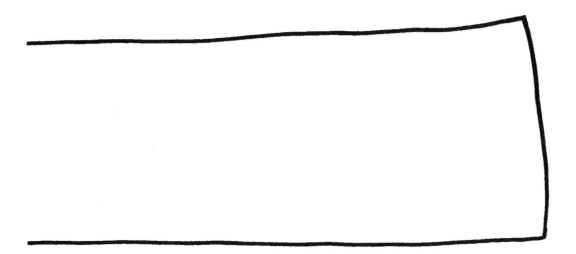

Trace all patterns
in reverse

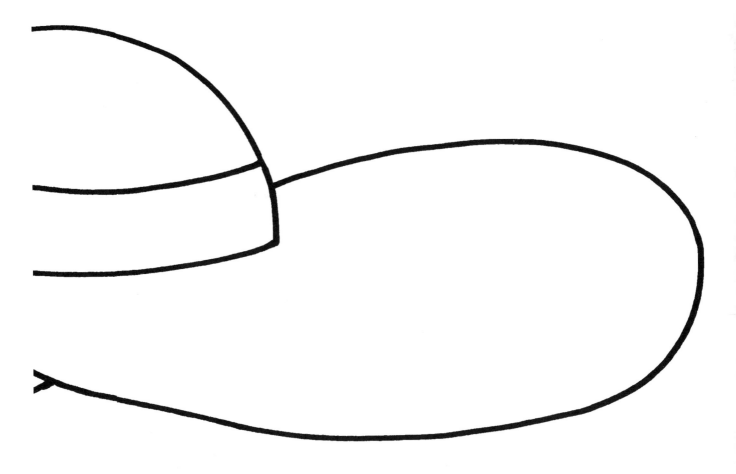

A Lady's Sampler

photo on page 15
patterns on pages 58 - 63

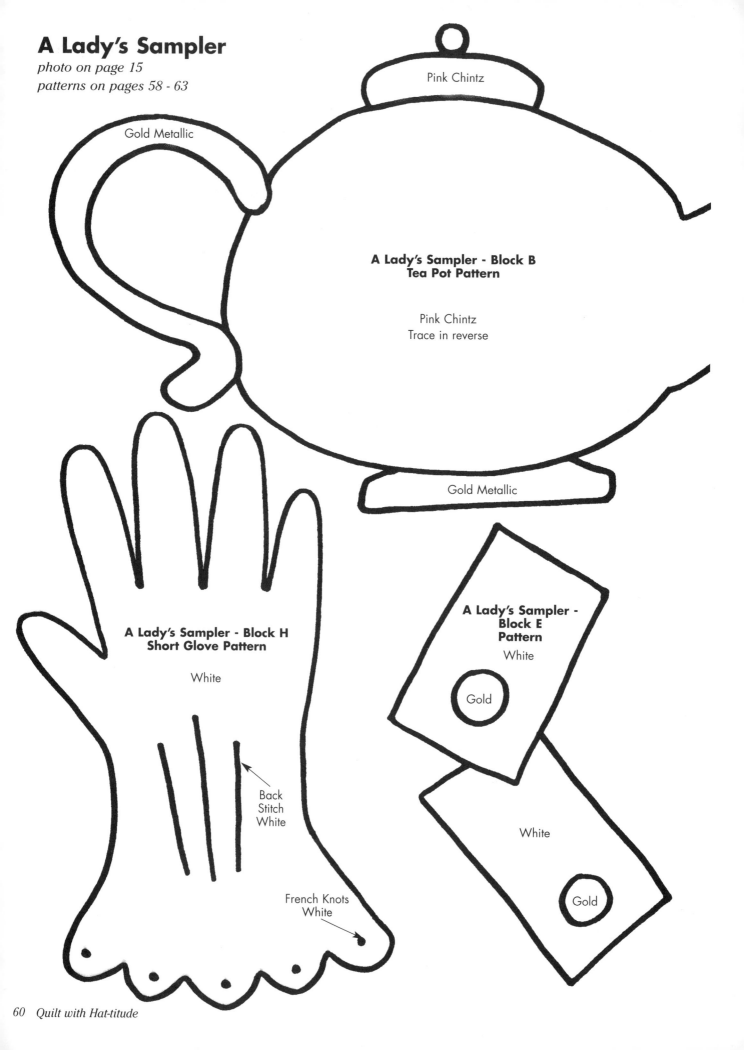

Pink Chintz

Gold Metallic

**A Lady's Sampler - Block B
Tea Pot Pattern**

Pink Chintz
Trace in reverse

Gold Metallic

**A Lady's Sampler - Block H
Short Glove Pattern**

White

Back
Stitch
White

French Knots
White

**A Lady's Sampler -
Block E
Pattern**

White

Gold

White

Gold

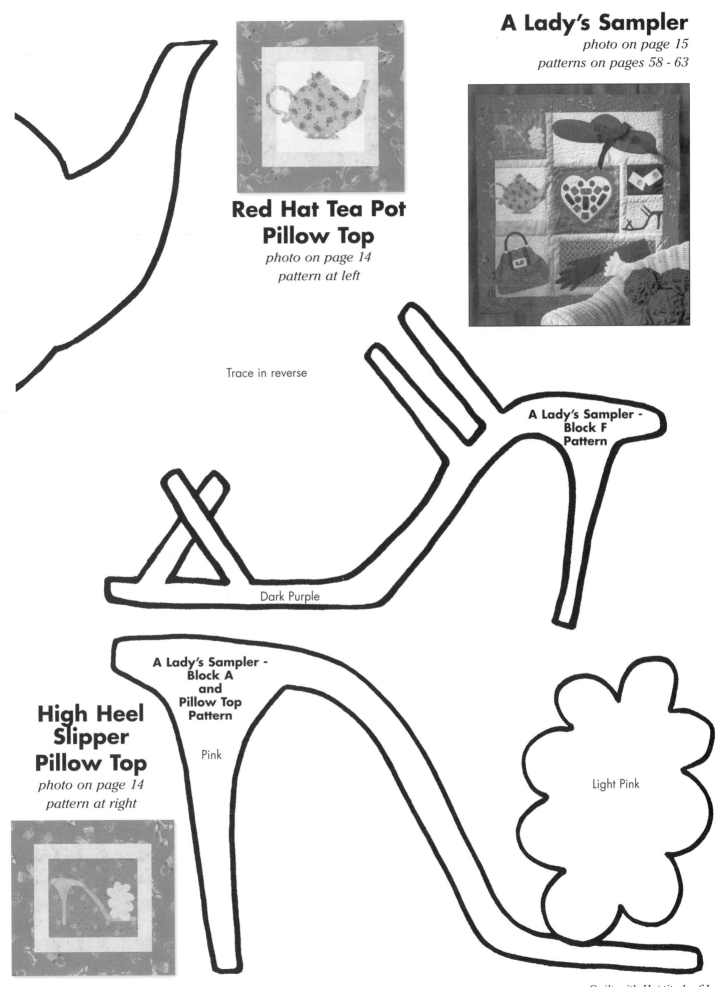

A Lady's Sampler

photo on page 15
patterns on pages 58 - 63

Red Hat Tea Pot
Pillow Top

photo on page 14
pattern at left

Trace in reverse

**A Lady's Sampler -
Block F
Pattern**

Dark Purple

**A Lady's Sampler -
Block A
and
Pillow Top
Pattern**

Pink

High Heel
Slipper
Pillow Top

photo on page 14
pattern at right

Light Pink

A Lady's Sampler

photo on page 15
patterns on pages 58 - 63

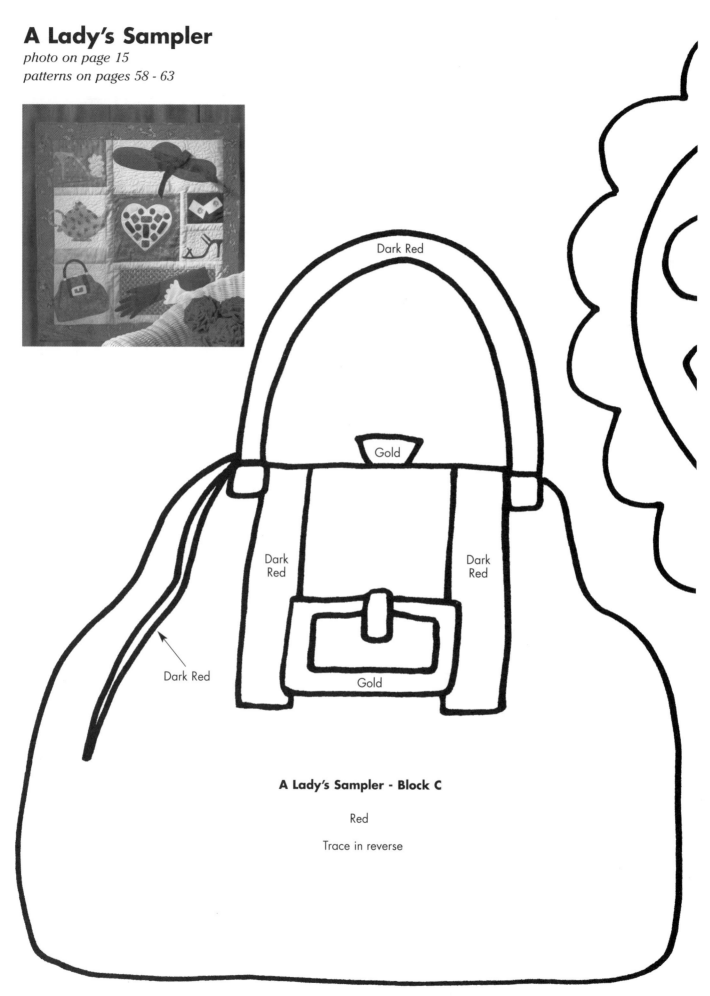

Dark Red

Gold

Dark
Red

Dark
Red

Dark Red

Gold

A Lady's Sampler - Block C

Red

Trace in reverse

A Lady's Sampler
photo on page 15
patterns on pages 58 - 63

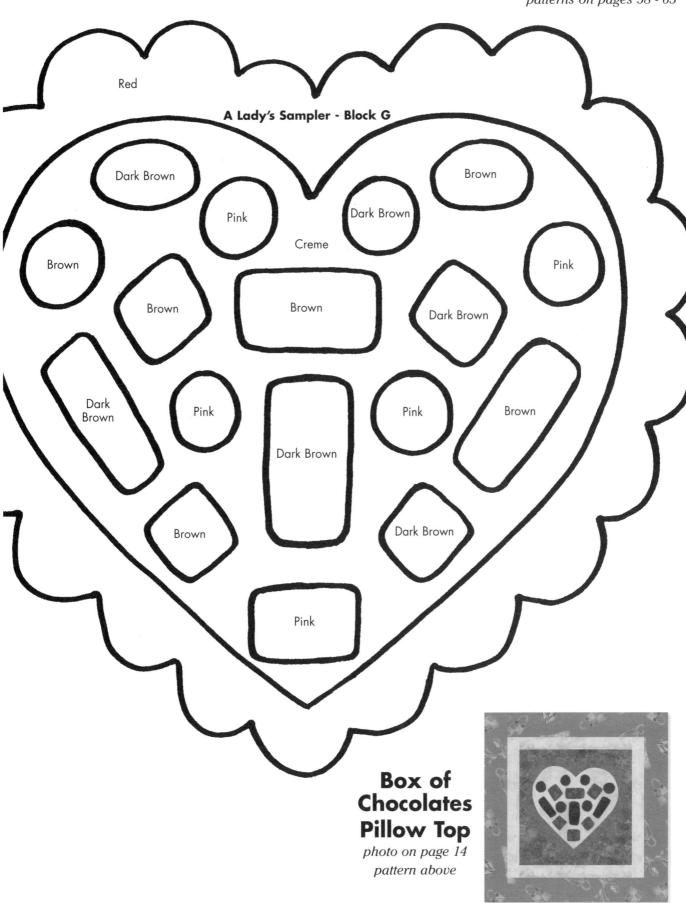

A Lady's Sampler - Block G

Red

Dark Brown

Brown

Pink

Dark Brown

Creme

Brown

Pink

Brown

Brown

Dark Brown

Pink

Dark Brown

Pink

Brown

Dark Brown

Pink

Brown

Dark Brown

Pink

Box of Chocolates Pillow Top

photo on page 14
pattern above

It's All About the HAT!

A hat for this,
A hat for that,
Nothing to wear,
Imagine that!

~ Sarah Haynes

Ah, Sweetheart don't you know
What I am driving at?
Why, my love for you is as big
As—your MERRY WIDOW HAT.

Copyright 1908
by I. Grollman

HOW DO THE BIG HATS STRIKE YOU?

"Manners are a sensitive awareness of the feeling of others. If you have that awareness, you have good manners, no matter what fork you use."
~ Emily Post

"Backward, turn backward, o time in your flight; make me a child again just for tonight."
~ Elizabeth Akers Allen

"If you obey all the rules, you miss all the fun." ~ Katherine Hepburn

"I come from a home where gravy is a beverage." ~ Erma Bombeck

"It's never too late in fiction or in life.
~ Nancy Thayer

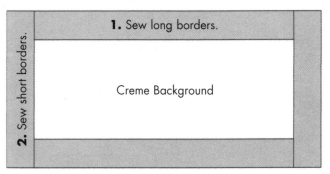

Watering Can Table Runner Diagram

Watering Can Table Runner

photo on page 67
patterns on pages 48 - 49

FINISHED SIZE: 14" x 28"
MATERIALS:
¼ yard Purple for border and binding
⅓ yard of Creme fabric for background
¼ yard or scraps for applique: Pink, Red, Green, Gold

CUTTING:	Purple BORDERS:		BINDING:
Creme colored	Cut 2	2¼" x 24"	Cut 2
BACKGROUND:	2	2¼" x 14"	strips of
Cut one 10½" x 24"			2" x 40"

INSTRUCTIONS:
1. Sew the 24" side border strips to each side.
2. Sew the 14" end border strips to each end. Press.
3. Sew strips together to measure 92" for binding.

Watering Can Applique Colors

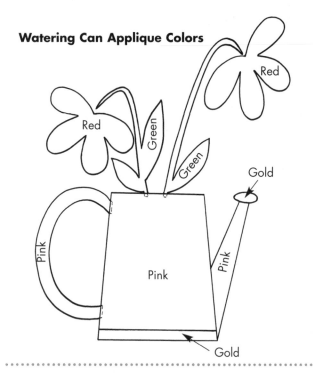

APPLIQUE:
1. Trace the applique patterns twice in reverse onto fusible web.
2. Label each piece. *Colors on runner are different from quilt.*
3. Press each drawn piece to fabric and cut out.
4. Watering can is Pink. Spout and bottom are Gold.
5. Flowers are Red. Stems and leaves are Green.
6. Use the pattern to position pieces on each end of the runner.
7. Press in place following your manufacturer's directions.
8. Follow the directions under "finishing up".

Finishing Up

5. Hand or machine quilt around each design.
6. Trim the edges in line with the quilt top.
7. Lay the binding face down along the front edge of the quilt top and pin.
8. Fold under the first ½" of the binding. See Diagram #1.
9. When you come to the corner, fold down, then up and pin. See Diagram #2.
10. Sew a ¼" seam all around the edge, overlapping the ends. See Diagram #3.
11. Fold over to the back and pin. Tuck under the edge and hand-stitch to secure.
12. Hand-stitch a dowel rod across the upper back for hanging.

I know everyone says "who looks at the back?" Believe me, people DO look at the back. I suggest you use a pretty fabric that complements the front of your project for your backing fabric. You'll be happy you did.

INSTRUCTIONS:
1. Lay the backing fabric face down on a table.
2. Lay the batting on top of the backing fabric, centered.
3. Lay the project on top of the batting and backing fabric.
4. Baste or use lots of pins to hold the three layers together.

Diagram 1

Diagram 2

Diagram 3

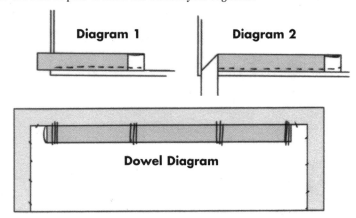

Dowel Diagram

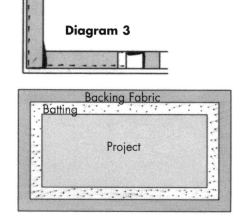

Watering cans are so romantic. Usually you find rusty old ones holding flower arrangements in gardens or on patios. Have fun making yours in happy spring colors.
patterns on page 46 - 47

Pour It On
Watering Can Table Runner

My thanks to those who helped on the projects in this book.

Cindy Kaufman - Machine Quilter • Betty Sheidegger - Seamstress
Sarah Haynes - Creative Assistant

Cheryl Haynes

MANY THANKS to my friends for their cheerful help and wonderful ideas!
- Kathy McMillan
- Jennifer Laughlin
- Donna Kinsey
- David & Donna Thomason

SUPPLIERS - Most craft and variety stores carry an excellent assortment of supplies.
If you need something special, ask your local store to contact the following companies:
BASIC SUPPLIES
 Warm Products, 800-234-9276, Seattle, WA (Warm & Natural cotton batting, Seam-A Seam fusible web)
 Hillcreek Designs, 619-562-5799, Santee, CA (Hand-dyed buttons)
FABRICS
 Benartex, 212-840-3250, New York, NY
 RJR, 800-422-5426, Torrance, CA
HAT & ACCESSORIES FABRICS
 Marcus Brothers Textiles, 212-519-0211, New York, NY

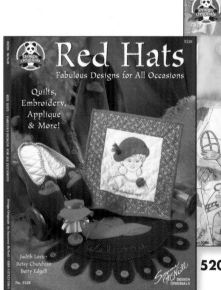

Whimsical Embroidery Kits

1815 - 1835
A fabulous
selection of over 20 kits for
Redwork or embroidery designs
with printed muslin, floss, buttons
and needle are available.

Cheryl Haynes

Cheryl Haynes is a talented designer. Her quilt patterns are popular across the country.

In this book Cheryl shares her love of color and whimsy with quilt, table runner and pillow designs featuring hats, shoes, purses, candy, gardening and all the necessary accessories.

For a brochure of her patterns, send $2.00 to: The Prairie Grove Peddler, 1568 Racine Avenue, Badger, Iowa 50516 or www.prairiegrovepeddler.com.

Hat-titude™

Additional Books on Quilting and Embroidery...

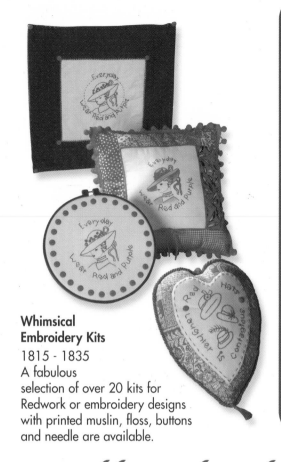

5226 Red Hats Book

5206 Ladies of Leisure

5202 Vintage Home

5152 Vintage Lin

0 23863 05227 6

ISBN

9 781574 215373

Design Originals
www.d-originals.com
2425 CULLEN STREET
FORT WORTH, TX 76107

Better Homes and Gardens®
teach yourself to
rotary-cut